TALES OF THE VILLAGE RABBI

A MANHATTAN CHRONICLE

E-Rights/E-Reads, Ltd. Publishers
171 East 74th Street, New York, NY 10021

www.ereads.com

TALES OF THE VILLAGE RABBI

A MANHATTAN CHRONICLE

BY RABBI HARVEY M. TATTELBAUM

E-Reads®

Dedicated with profound love to
My darling Meryl;
Adam Tattelbaum; Kate Gun; and Polly Schnell;
Their loved ones:
Nancy Rosenfeld; Howard Gun; and Gordon Schnell
And
Jack and Tess Tamar
Jesse and Emory Gun
And
Wynter, Rayn, and Quoya Schnell

————

And
Warm thanks from the author to
Leslie Curtis, Editor
Richard Curtis, Agent
And
Michael Gaudet of E-Reads, Publisher

CONTENTS

Introduction

IT was not a town in the Ukraine or Belarus, nor a shtetl in Poland or Lithuania, nor a shtiebele in Russia or Azerbaijan.

It has been a bustling, thriving village on the Island of Manhattan for over three hundred years. Its settlers and occupants were from all the nations of the earth.

As the population of the whole island grew, a line of demarcation became pronounced. It had no Yiddish, Hungarian, Russian or Polish tones to it—simply "14th Street"—the northern boundary. The southern boundary was vague and darted in and out of lower Manhattan, a boundary that touched Chinatown, Little Italy, the Lower East Side, the wholesale meat district—all venues of crowded, busy and unrelenting vitality.

Many who settled here felt a certain pride of residence—a pride that often kept them below 14th Street, if possible. A pride that allowed them to respond without any self-effacement to the question, "Where do you live?" and the quickly forthcoming answer was "Greenwich Village."

Land values in "The Village" have skyrocketed. Apartments are being rented or bought for prices that surpass the levels of many comparable Upper West Side and Upper East Side dwellings in Manhattan.

My years as part of "The Village" community were among the most exciting of my life. Many descendants of the ancient house of Israel settled there. Among the families I knew, some claimed residency back two or three or more generations (one, even back to the time of the Pilgrims of the 17th century).

The pride of being part of the inner and immediate life of "The Village" was an integral part of the worldview of many of my Jews. One found an easy acceptance among denizens of all that made "The Village" famous throughout the world: the art shows; the gay rights parades; the outrageous adult Halloween processions; the dousing in the fountain of NYU graduates at commencement-time; the community battles to keep NYU from expanding its libraries and learning centers; the illogical pattern of crisscrossing charm-filled streets; the crowded stores and eating places; the constant hordes of tourists and passers-through; the beggars and homeless; the high-cost brownstones and the imposing new apartment buildings; St. Vincent's Hospital; the Fashion Institute; the New School and the private schools; the centuries-old fabulously wealthy churches; the old clubs—and for me, above all, the gathering places of the Jewish community. One, in particular, on 12th Street between University Place and Broadway: Congregation B'nai Israel of Greenwich Village. Though not the only synagogue in the area, under its better-known title as "The Village Temple," it enabled me to claim the title of "Village Rabbi." That was where I explored, served and led for an era of my life that I cannot ever put out of my mind.

That was where I worked—and these are some of my stories.

A Bracha For A Bike

I RECALL that the day was sunny, cool, and beautiful. I had sat down at my desk to return phone calls and write some letters and my rabbi's article for our temple publication. I was well into my agenda when the intercom buzzed. The temple secretary informed me that a person was here to see me on an important matter.

In my entire career I never turned anyone away who did not have an appointment.

A gentle knock on the door followed—and in walked the most handsome, the most beautiful man I had ever seen. He was dressed in leather from head to toe—except that his leather cap was in his hand. It was not old creased leather—it was shiny and a bit stiff. I could hear leathery brittleness as he moved closer to my desk. He had a luminous smile that lit up my study and a smile that simply radiated a pearliness rarely seen. He also seemed extraordinarily friendly and sweetly naïve.

I shook his hand and introduced myself. In his haste to get to his important matter, he overlooked giving me his name.

He got right to the point: "Rabbi, would you please bless my new motorcycle?"

I was a bit stunned. I had never blessed any kind of machine before. I didn't really want to. I couldn't help but react cynically in days gone by to the big churches in town that blessed pets and other animal companions—or Bishops who blessed the recreation and fishing boats at the docks of the Hudson and elsewhere.

But there was something so guileless, so ingenuous about him and the way he asked for the blessing. It was not in me to say "no."

I answered that I would bless him-a living human being-but not his motorcycle, an inanimate object. I would wish for the best for him: for sunny days and happy journeys, for strength, good judgment, good fortune, and good health. But I could not bless his motorcycle.

"Please," he asked, "come downstairs and see it." I was happy to go with him. In spite of the fact that his gleaming, shiny bike, with every possible chrome feature added to it, was in my parking spot in front of the Temple entrance (I often came to work by subway), I had to admit it, his motorcycle was an object of beauty. One could feel the love, the handwork, the care, the elbow grease, the polish lavished upon it.

"You see," he said, "it lives!"

Something deep in my own animist soul agreed, but my rationalist Weltanschauung won out. I put my hand upon his shoulder. I blessed him as kindly and as lovingly as I could. I even put my other hand on his gleaming, inanimate, "significant other"-and ended with a moment of silent prayer before the final "amain." When I had finished and informally wished him all kinds of good luck and happy riding, he climbed on the vehicle with a look of pride and satisfaction. He started up—a deep roaring, reverberating sound (probably illegal for the city)—and gunned it in neutral a few times. Above the din, he shouted, "Thanks Rabbi!" and roared off on 12th Street into the sunset.

I couldn't help but smile. I never saw him again. When I see gleaming "bikes" along the highways, I am reminded of the "wonder" of 12th street! It was a fitting jump-start for the Rabbi in the Village.

Of Broken Glass

WHEN I first came to New York City with my wife, I served as an Assistant Rabbi at a large east side uptown congregation. The position had a mandatory termination after the third year.

I went through all the proper protocol of placement and was engaged to serve the Village Temple on East 12th Street. I always felt that it would be beneficial professionally to live near the temple.

With the oncoming birth of our first son followed by our first daughter, we did not plan to move. The commute was easy and quick. Our apartment on East 86th Street was not far from the Lexington Avenue subway line, and both East 86th Street and East 14th Street were express stops.

Although the subway ride was convenient, we still eventually planned to move downtown. We looked at many places. "Spiritually" we had already moved but "physically" we conducted a constant search. We found one apartment on lower Fifth Avenue that was truly lovely and held great possibilities for our growing family. That apartment was large, with rooms of outstanding size in an old apartment building designed by the famous architect Stanford White.

A prominent couple from the congregation lived in that building, the wife a noted judge and her husband a well-known attorney.

When I asked the lawyer his opinion about the building, he answered that yes, it was a beautiful, distinctive building, he and his wife had been living there for years, and the rodent and vermin infestation was not too bad a problem! A quick "thank you" for his kindness brought our search to an abrupt end.

It always bothered me that we weren't successful in settling near the temple. But it was especially bothersome when I received a phone call at about 9:00 p.m. one evening a few days before the High Holy Days. A member of the temple, Tina, lived in the building right next door to the synagogue. Her voice was filled with panic. "Rabbi, the Temple has been broken into. The glass from the front door is all over the street!"

I rang the president of the schul, who lived on West 12th Street and told him of the report. He, in turn, called the police. I immediately ran to the 86th Street subway station and caught the express train for 14th Street. I was at the Temple door in a matter of minutes. I got there even before the president and the police, who arrived moments later.

The police officer reported that indeed, shards of heavy plate glass from the sturdy door were all over the sidewalk and those who "broke and entered" must be well on their way. A strong strain of doubt within me caused me to disagree with the cop. In logical rabbinic fashion, I could not help but "size-up" the situation Talmudically. I said, "Look, the door is locked. All the broken glass from the door is on the street and there's none inside the entryway. The hole is too small for human exit. *So we must conclude that whoever did this is still inside!*"

My logic predominated and I unlocked the remnants of the front door. After entering we saw the large metal tape-holder used to smash the glass from the inside. Upon inspection, the policeman agreed with my conclusion. "Yes, whoever did this is still in here," he said as he drew his pistol from the holster.

We started up the stairs, very slowly, the cop with the gun drawn, the president with the pale face, and I, bringing up the rear. What a sight that procession must have been! Marines storming the beachhead; advance Rangers scaling the cliffs. One detail remains in my mind to complete this picture, that the cop walking up the stairs step-by-step seemed somewhat bow-legged, but alert, gun drawn, and very quiet, slow step by slow step.

We turned the corner to the well lit meeting room and the policeman's voice sounded from inside the temple office: "WHAT THE HELL ARE YOU DOING HERE?"

Both the president and I followed the policeman in. Sitting at the temple secretary's desk was a very dejected, quiet, upset middle-aged man.

Our intruder was not innocent, but was not motivated by malicious intent. He looked very sad and pitiable in Elsa the secretary's chair. He said he entered the Temple because the door was unlocked. It had been unlocked because the choir had been rehearsing for the High Holy Days in the sanctuary downstairs. He admitted that he had used the phone and had made some calls to his family in Puerto Rico. But he made those calls only after he tried to leave and discovered the door was now locked and bolted. The choir, cantor and organist must have finished the rehearsal and left, locking the door behind them from the outside. He did smash the door, but could only crack open a portion of the heavy plate glass. He was a prisoner, locked in, and could not get out. He went back upstairs and communicated with his world, his hemisphere, on our temple phone.

The three Marine/Ranger/Rescue/Warriors reasoned it all out step by step. The policeman was very positive and forceful. "Don't press charges! It would all be a pitiful waste of time. No malicious intent could be proved. The case would simply be thrown out and an overloaded judicial system would do nothing but fritter away the valuable time of a busy Rabbi, his president, and a local law enforcement officer!"

After hearing a few heartfelt harangues in this direction, the president and I agreed with the policeman. Insurance would cover the damage to the door.

But before we let the intruder go, the policeman did his share for justice: he removed his revolver from the holster again. He moved it from side to side, punctuating the words he delivered to the miscreant in the loudest voice I have ever heard:

"DON'T YOU EVER COME HERE AGAIN. IF I EVER CATCH YOU NEAR THIS PLACE, IT WILL BE THE END OF YOU!"

An echo of "The Voice" of Sinai?

The return ride uptown was much slower than the trip downtown.

"One Should Cleave Unto the Other"

WHEN all the meetings concerning my engagement as the Village Temple Rabbi had ended, I promised the officers of the congregation that I would officially report to work on the 15th of August. Although the "city never sleeps," it truly does quiet down somewhat in the month of August. It was hot, humid, grimy and, in some ways, deserted. But with a great deal of excitement and enthusiasm, I was in early to begin the work of my new position. Later on in the day, the secretary informed me that a number of the officers had called in to make sure I had arrived as promised.

I had hardly put away some of my books on the shelf of my new study when the phone rang. A couple wished to come by that very day to arrange a wedding ceremony for the following day. When they arrived shortly after, they had all necessary documents. Both were Jewish and very eager to be married. Only the bride's parents would be present as witnesses. The groom wore a dark suit and tie and she a simple dress; they were modest in appearance. Pleasant and forthcoming, they answered my innocent questions readily. All seemed well.

We set the ceremony for 2:00 p.m. the following day. The parents would sign the civil marriage license, and the Temple secretary and a neighbor of the Synagogue would sign as witnesses to the Jewish wedding document, the Ketubah.

When 1:45 p.m. came, the bride, the groom and her parents arrived. I welcomed them into my study. The bride's appearance was very different from the day before. Relatively thin, she had dark, dark eyes and jet-black hair, at least what could be seen of it. Now most of her head was covered by some kind of indescribable head covering, a cross between a "babushka" and an old-fashioned pilot's helmet. It was white and clung to her head and was covered with decorative pieces of cloth strips that stuck out like the whiskers of a cat all over her skull. The overall affect was Medusa-like. But the hat was less obtrusive than her jet-black dress, which was short and had a cleavage designed to be bare from her neck to below her breasts. Her breasts were enormous. Perhaps they seemed even more so because of her basically thin body. One could not help but be slightly mesmerized by their size and protrusion; I did my best to keep looking at her eyes.

The groom, however, did not fare as well. Although the day before he had seemed at ease, on this his wedding day, he had a constant facial tic. It seemed that every time he looked at her, his glance slipped down to her striking cleavage, which resulted in four or five blinks, as if the sight was just too much of an ocular challenge for his vision.

Her parents seemed not to notice a thing, and were ready, calm, and utterly silent. All amenities were completed and I led them to the sanctuary downstairs. There were too few people for a chupah. I asked them all to ascend the bimah. As was my practice, I was just about to open the curtain of the ark, but something in me held me back, as if a divine force within me had put on the brakes. I do not believe in any kind of anthropomorphism in reference to God, but my inner naive conception suddenly felt that if the deity were present he/she would not be able to help him/herself and would also start blinking like the groom, in an uncontrollable tic-like fashion before that formidable visual pectoral onslaught. I did not open the ark, but conducted the ceremony while keeping my eyes as high as I could on the foreheads of the bride and groom.

When the ceremony came to its conclusion, the groom took another look at his bride. His eyes blinked out of control, and his foot missed the glass I had placed on the floor in front of him. He tried again, but made the mistake of looking at her the instant before he tried. He blinked involuntarily and missed again. The third time, he simply turned away totally—his eyes on the pulpit chair to the right of the ark, away from the direction of his bride. He hit the target, broke it, and I urged him to kiss his bride. As he did so, the blinking was no longer sporadic, but constant.

Congratulations and "mazel-tovs" were offered all around. The bride and her parents left the sanctuary holding hands. Her groom brought up the rear of the small procession. I pictured him blinking the length of 12th Street, and off into the sunset, until that day when he might become accustomed to one of nature's unique phenomena.

As I climbed the stairs leading back to my study, I realized I was blinking. Was it memory? Tension? Empathy? "Stop it!" I said sharply to myself in a tone that momentarily frightened my secretary, and I was cured.

Even as I recall the ceremony, my eyes seem to want to blink to ease the tension.

The Interview

IWAS born in Boston, raised in Boston, educated in Boston and then spent most of my life in New York City.

I personify a commonly stated notion: one can take the boy out of Boston, but one cannot take the enthusiasm for Boston basketball out of the boy. In the years of my maturation the Celtics became the most successful team in the history of American sports.

Some of us played ball whenever and wherever we could: before; after; and (sometimes) during classes, especially at the Hebrew College which was for so many of us "school after school" every day except Friday and Saturday and Sunday mornings. Class-time basketball was forbidden once the Dean (a famous Hebrew poet) was hit in the head by a straying pass during class hours.

The love of basketball came with me to my Navy Chaplaincy in the Marine Corps where we played some very rough games at lunchtime, and followed me to the 92nd Street "Y" on Manhattan's Upper East Side.

The games at the "Y" were also very rough and strenuous. There were many players and limited time and courts. In order to play a good amount of time, one's "pick-up" team had to win. If you won, you could play again . . . and again . . . and again. If you lost, you were essentially done for the evening. I loved playing. Fortunately, there were more days of extended playing than days of early elimination. It often came to pass when I was an Assistant Rabbi and my Senior Rabbi was leading services or preaching (I have *never* admitted this to anyone, till now), I would sometimes replay the highlights of the exciting games in my mind. It was challenging and fun to listen attentively and to ruminate athletically.

Strangely, basketball helped me attain my next position, as solo Rabbi of the Village Temple.

I remember the interview well. First, the Search Committee took me to a charming restaurant for an excellent dinner at "Il Bambino" on 12th Street and University Place. After dinner we went to the small social hall of the temple where the entire Board of Trustees interviewed me.

I was asked question after question. I admit that I always enjoyed being interviewed. Ego-trips are enticing. I was delighted to respond to their questions about me, my background, my resume, my experience, my education and, particularly, my theology. I took special delight in the last topic because I felt that in many ways I was breaking new ground. For me, Judaism included a spiritual, philosophical, religious humanism, terms that are neither mutually exclusive nor redundant to me.

One does *not* have to believe in a "personal" conception of God. If anything, the tortured history of the Jewish people of the last two thousand years belied a personal "Providence" that listens to prayer and that watches over us and protects us. Living in the post-Holocaust period was vivid proof that we were on our own in an indifferent universe.

For me, what we mean by God was the unknown, the x-factor, the mystery, the hoped-for beauty and answer, the unimaginable creative power that brought life into being. Reaching out to it in appropriate community prayer, song, and poetry helped to make us, I believe, a community of people who are sensitive, caring seekers of knowledge, truth and compassion.

I wanted to expound upon these points, but "basketball" became an obstacle. The richest man in the Congregation (so I later learned, the founder and CEO of "New York Metals" and, wouldn't you know it, a recent winner of an enormous Irish Sweepstakes prize from a ticket sold to him by another Board Member) asked me what kind of physical activities I did during my spare time. I told them of my delight in playing basketball. Many joined in on this topic. Where did I play? Was it full court or half-court? Was it three-man, five-man? Was it shirts vs. skin? How often did I play? What position did I play? Would I continue to play?

I wanted to talk theology, but they seemed unanimously conspired to talk basketball. The New York Knicks as in many other seasons were terrible that year and the Village Temple leaders almost masochistically elicited from me my expression of awe of the (then) constantly triumphant Boston Celtics. They expressed their dream for the Celtics to play in and for New York City.

As it turned out, they did elect a Boston Celtic fan to become their rabbi for the next six years.

The Great Wedding Robbery

(Otherwise, It Was A Splendid Ceremony)

WE had learned our lesson at the Village Temple and learned it well: the front door should be kept locked if the entrance was not guarded, and that is what we did. Until the day we had a wedding on a Sunday afternoon. And Sunday was el Domingo! On el Domingo our custodian, Pedro, did not work even though Sunday was a day when he might be most needed.

The wedding was scheduled for 1:00 p.m. and nearly everyone invited was present. Unfortunately, *nearly* meant not *all*. I was scheduled to officiate alone. As I was about to lock our infamous front door, the bride especially pleaded with me to leave it open. Some of her dearest relatives and friends had not yet come. I was reluctant to do so—but who can resist the pleadings of a bride on the day of her wedding? Fully confident of the benevolence of the universe, I left the door unlocked.

The other request I happily fulfilled was to start the ceremony exactly on time. I was about one-third of the way into the ceremony, mesmerizing the attendant congregation with my poetic words of hope and endearment, when my heart started racing madly. Two men came through the unlocked door. Their hair was long and curly, in what are called dred-locks. On this chilly day, they had no outer clothing beyond light, colorful short-sleeved shirts and rather splotched, tight-fitting dark jeans. They entered and saw all the coats on the hooks on the side wall of the lobby leading to the sanctuary. Since I faced the gathering, while all others were facing the ark, I was the only one who saw them. Across the distance of the cozy sanctuary, our "jewel of a schul," our eyes met. I saw their faces as they sized up the situation. They knew I was in the middle of a ceremony. Their glances almost dared me to cry out as they spread out their long arms and gathered in every coat and bag hanging on those hooks. I could feel my chest thumping inside my shirt and suit jacket. They had essentially "dared" me and I could not ruin the ceremony. Yet I could not let them get away with their criminal gall.

I called for silent prayer. I asked that we close our eyes and pray with all our hearts' intensity for the well being of the bride and groom. I slithered to the back of the sanctuary. "I shall only be a moment," I said as I exited to the lobby, out the front door and raced across the street. On the other side of the street was an auxiliary police station, where New York's "finest" came for special training, classes, and seminars. I had often eyed the building with envy as I thought it would make a great Hebrew school. But no such thoughts were in my mind at that moment. I opened the front door, still wearing my tallit and yarmulke. There was a guard at the door. I explained as fast as I could: "I'm the Rabbi from the temple across the street. I'm in the middle of a wedding ceremony. Two men came in and stole all the coats and handbags. Help us. Do something!"

I felt certain that he thought I was a crazy man. I also felt sure that the entire wedding party must have thought I had gone mad. What kind of a Rabbi leaves the Synagogue in the middle of a wedding ceremony? When I returned and was walking down the aisle I announced with acute tremolo in my voice: "Friends, all the coats and bags have been stolen. I have already given word to the police. What we must do now is the most important thing we can do: finish the ceremony! This is what we must do!"

As I was talking, there were muffled shrieks, sighs of agony, whispers, and yelps. But I took my place before the ark facing the bride and groom. "120 over 80" must long ago have turned into "300 over 200" for all of us. With utmost restraint I continued and finished the ceremony. In spite of it all, everyone seemed attentive. There was tremendous release and relief when the groom broke the glass and kissed the bride. As the two folded into one before me, my view of the street beyond the lobby was unhindered. Something was going on outside the door. I could not be sure, and proceeded back up the aisle to see what was happening. Everyone in the wedding party followed. Although East 12th Street is a one-way street, police cars were coming from both directions. Inside one of the cars were the two thieves *and* all the coats and handbags. Uniformed officers began distributing the belongings. There was laughter, relief, and a sense of triumph, victory.

I felt compelled to thrust my head into the car where the two men sat and to proclaim aloud: "How can you rob a synagogue in the middle of a wedding? How do you dare do such a thing?" I paused. They both spoke but it was such a mumbled mumbo-jumbo I couldn't grasp a word of what they said.

One of the policemen said that he saw the two men walking very quickly along Union Square, about two blocks from the Temple. Their arms were filled with coats and bags. He said he knew immediately that the picture was wrong and they were up to no good, and at that moment the radio call came in about a robbery in a synagogue on 12th Street during a ceremony. Other cars were alerted and converged in front of the front door of the Temple.

I later learned that the people for whom we had left the door open never did show up. But once the goods were returned, the wedding party went on its merry way.

Much later on, perhaps a year, or more . . .

My wife and I were "shpatzeering", wandering the Village and browsing on a rare day off. There was a store with some amazing material, huge slabs of gigantic South American jungle trees polished and lacquered to shining perfection. The large store was filled with these creations and they were quite striking. Some were fashioned into large tables, end tables, coffee tables, clocks—whatever the creative imagination and a talented hand could fashion.

Behold, the proprietor of the store was a handsome, tall, mustachioed, man. I knew him—recognition came quickly! He was the groom on the day of the great wedding robbery. We acknowledged each other. We laughed and embraced. What a ceremony! Something we could never forget! How is your bride? How are you doing?

The answer came forth in short order: "We were divorced some time ago. The divorce had nothing to do with the tumultuous wedding ceremony. The ceremony was one we would always remember!"

The Divine Element in Human Affairs

COMPASSION. That is the central purpose of a religious institution. Compassion—of the heart, the mind, the hand. The transmission of the notion that in this religious place there will be those emotions that sympathize, empathize, support ... that even if no solutions can be found there is a heart and soul that cares, that listens. "I support you—even though I cannot really help you." My caring listening, my extended hand, my own tear, my embrace—all that can help in its modest way, and is among the first and highest purposes of a house of worship and study.

The proffering of compassion is more important than any rules and traditions, more important than ancient mandates, more important than expounding about God. Compassion is the divine element in human affairs, and sometimes the source of compassion can be very surprising. So a tale of compassion in a Village "that does not sleep."

The Bar Mitzvah boy and his father came to see me. All details had already been worked out. It was a special meeting to prepare for the day. The boy's mother? Yes, she was coming to the ceremony. The biological parents had been divorced long ago and the father had long since remarried. His wife, the Bar Mitzvah's stepmother, had taken care of all the details. She had done so lovingly and efficiently. She would be recognized as the mother of the household. The boy's biological mother had been institutionalized for years. There was only rare contact between her and her only son, rare contact with all the rest of her family. The illness was beyond her doing. She had not experimented with drugs or alcohol. She was not an addict. An arduous, years-long investigation in hindsight had confirmed her mental failing as genetic and basically untreatable, untreatable only until the discovery of tranquilizers. She could be tranquilized but not cured. The Bar Mitzvah boy was her only child and she was coming to the ceremony with an aide. She did not want to sit on the bimah with her son; she wanted only to be there, present in the congregation and as unobtrusive as possible. She wanted to be part of this special happy time in her son's life.

This did not distress the father, son, and stepmother. They simply felt that I should know. They knew that it was right and they felt, as did I, that it would work out. They gave me permission to alert the volunteer ushers should anything go awry. We trusted that all would go well, and thankfully it did.

Although I had never met the woman before, I could tell exactly who she was in the congregation. She was not just there—she was *intensely there*. She was very pretty. She was tastefully and modestly dressed. No one outside the realm of confidentiality would have known that the attractive young woman in the fifth row was severely ill. I could see and feel her holding back her tears (not totally successfully). I could literally touch the aura of love that she radiated. Her pride was obvious and her joy deeply touching. The ceremony went smoothly. The boy performed his chanting and readings without fault. It was a success for the boy, a triumph for the family.

After it was over, the boy's mother came to me. With tangible emotion she told me tearfully that she had never been so happily moved. She felt she had been part of something wonderful. But she had to leave right away; it was too much for her to attend the reception. She seemed relieved that she had gotten this far. Could she, please, take something with her, something that would help her continue to live the moment that had tapped the wellspring of love of her inner being, something that was part of her son, the synagogue, the wonderful moment? Could she buy and take with her the prayer book she had used during the service?

Without hesitation I told her I would be honored for the synagogue and myself to give her the book. It was our pleasure to do so. It was hers and I wished her continuing enjoyment. The emotion welled up—but no tears. One could feel them trickling inside. In no way would she let herself bring sadness and loss of control to this day of joy.

She put on her coat and with her aide quickly left the synagogue. They got into a cab to go to the airport and return to wherever "home" was.

The day passed. I appeared briefly at the reception and then made my way home. By mid-evening my telephone rang. It was the boy's mother in a state of profound distress. As she had transferred from the taxi to the airport terminal, somehow the prayer book was lost. She looked in every pocket and every corner of her bags. It was not to be found. I told her not to be upset, I would send her another as quickly as possible. That would be lovely, she told me, but she wanted the one she held, the one into which her occasional uncontrollable tears had fallen. She would live with whatever I sent, but could not help but mourn her clumsiness and her loss. I tried to comfort her. Perhaps some of my own empathy did come through, but nothing could have given her the balm she needed.

At 11:30 that night the telephone rang again. It was a man's voice, with a thick foreign accent. He gave his name: long, multi-syllabic, Mediterranean. He explained that he was a taxi driver. It had been a busy day and night. He was sorry to disturb me but couldn't wait and apologized for not calling sooner.

There were a few airport pick-ups and the Saturday theatre rush.

He had picked up two women in his cab in the early afternoon. One woman clutched a book, held it to her face and looked through it intensely. She then held it to her heart with her eyes closed. She opened a page and smiled as she showed something in it to the woman next to her.

When they reached La Guardia, the airport was crowded. Taxis were honking. The police were pushing. Horns were blaring. People were arriving and departing. In the midst of parking and getting the luggage, the book was left behind. He knew it was important. When he got home later that night he saw the words: "Property of the Village Temple." He looked up the number. He called. The answering machine said that in an emergency the Rabbi should be called. He did so. Would the Temple be open tomorrow? Sunday was another workday and he knew he would be downtown. Yes, the Temple would be open (God Bless Sunday School). Give the book to anyone there and say it is for the Rabbi.

I could not express enough gratitude to this kindly man. He would take no payment for any inconvenience. He knew it was important and he wanted only to do his good deed, to do the right thing. "If only there were more human beings like you in our world." He was grateful for my reaction.

I called the mother. The telephone system was closed. The call would have to wait till the morning. I called as early as was possible. I could feel the renewed joy zinging through the long-distance miles. She said that no one could ever know what happiness she felt over her good luck. She would try never again to lose faith in herself or others. She would soften her brittle anger against herself and the world. The special day and the amazing return of the prayer book would always be a touchstone of strength.

I wish I knew where she might be now, or the whereabouts of her son, or the cabbie. I felt deeply certain that a moment of compassion lingered for a long time to come in their minds and hearts. It did in mine.

The Conversion
of Shayna

OCCASIONALLY it helps to start at the end of the story.
Some events that take place in a Rabbi's life must remain
confidential. The category of information that is called "privileged
communication" is well known. The law protects a clergyman from
divulging private information to anyone, except in dire circumstances;
otherwise it must never be done.

But in the case of "Shayna", and the end of my tale, it was there for
the whole world to see: her bosom that seemed to flow off the page in
Playboy Magazine. (Of course, I didn't *buy* one! Someone, who knew
us both, sent me a copy.)

When I first met her, it was on a rainy, cold day in Greenwich
Village. She lived up to all the credentials ascribed to a Village denizen.
She was cute, but very scrawny—a scrawniness made more sharp by
the rather ratty, totally wet, fake fur coat she was wrapped in when she
entered the Temple. She was beautifully spoken, wonderfully educated,
quite impoverished, cogently expressive, and a self-admitted user of
"pot" and LSD. LSD, like its chief proponent Dr. Timothy Leary, was
at the height of its notoriety at that time.

Shayna was married to a Jewish man and wanted to convert to
Judaism. She claimed she was completely ready to do so. In a number of
flights of drug-induced illusion, she had found God several times. She
waxed poetic and eloquent when she described her "spiritual journeys."

I did not doubt her sincerity. I believe that she spoke with truth and
heart. I told her that I would accept her as a student for instruction in

Judaism on only one condition: that she stop using drugs during this time period. She promised she would cease.

She came to my study many times, attended special classes, did all the assigned reading—and more. She attended Shabbat and festival services. She even had a few titles to suggest to me. Every now and then I caught a hint of advocacy from her that taking drugs would be a good experience for me. I never took the suggestion but from time to time kept reminding her of her promise. Her husband came with her to a number of our meetings. He was quiet and shy, but seemed pleased and comfortable with the process and the experience.

Shayna delved into her Jewish studies with enthusiasm. She appreciated the history of the Jewish people and seemed to identify strongly with the phrase "a daughter of Israel." She loved the story of Ruth and her conversion to Judaism about 2,500 years ago. She was enthralled by the allusion that Ruth, a convert to Judaism, would become the great-grandmother of King David, the greatest of all the kings of ancient Israel from whose descendancy the Messiah would be born and rise.

Her passion for learning was exemplary and she flourished as a student. I felt very pleased to carry out all the rituals of conversion with her and for her.

By the time she officially became a "daughter of the House of Israel" she was quite pregnant. The scrawniness did not disappear, but was supplemented by the natural fullness of a woman only a few months from the time of birth. She had a glowing look of radiance, as some women do.

While pregnant and out taking a walk in the streets of our "Village", she was approached by two men. They were thrilled by the way she looked. They were ecstatic when they posed the question concerning singing and musical ability and acting experience and she answered, "Yes!" Yes, she could read music; yes, she had acted in high school and college; yes, she loved to sing.

Pending an audition, they offered her a part in a musical play that they were producing. She got the part. She had some major singing in the production. After a modest beginning in a Village theatre, the play hit Broadway quickly and became one of the most outstanding, long-lasting hits in the history of the Broadway Theatre (recently revived again to great popularity and acclaim)!

Not long into the role Playboy Magazine approached her, asking her to pose nude. She agreed, and that scrawny, rain-dampened, ratty fake fur—enwrapped villager's bosom became the visual property of all America. Her engorged breasts seemed to roll off the page.

I was present at her apartment when her eight-day old son was circumcised. Her place was an "ancient" walk-up. There was no furniture. She was comfortable with her son on a mattress on the floor. The 2-1/2 rooms were filled with people from the neighborhood and the cast. The mohel did his work efficiently and only a few theater performances were missed.

My wife and I went to see her on Broadway. She really was very good. The play made a tremendous impression on me and I thought about it for days. The music was advanced and electrifying. The message was agonized and profound. An enormous part of our lives is devoted to a search for meaning and for purpose, especially in a complicated, often deeply troubled world, a world in which war and terrible violence make ineradicable imprints upon our consciousness.

We went backstage to congratulate her. She was thrilled to see us. She said she felt particularly radiant on stage that night. She was right.

I regret that the only time I saw her since then was when she appeared in a television commercial selling some sort of skin cream.

I had heard unofficially that eventually she and her husband divorced, but I didn't think much about her until a mutual acquaintance sent us the rather eye-popping copy of her Playboy Magazine exposure.

I always had the suspicion that during the course of study she did not keep her promise about taking drugs and in those days there were few warnings about pregnancy complications from anything.

I did not think it appropriate to keep her photograph among my personal mementos that included Kiddush cups, menorahs, mezuzot, and plaques.

The Binding of Mickey

"He who steals a person—whether to sell or hold shall be put to death."

Exodus Chapter 5, Verse 16.

THE capacity of human beings to perpetrate evil doings was the furthest thing from my mind on a peaceful springtime late morning when I arrived at my study following a long and joyous Temple Passover Seder the evening before. The truth was that I didn't even have to come in. But the Passover Seders and services, punctuated by Shabbat and numerous ritual and pastoral duties, created a backlog of messages and needed responses.

I felt fully relaxed and at ease. The outer phone rang and the Temple secretary informed me that a strange-sounding call was for me.

I took the call, and its impact was indelible on both my family and me for the rest of our lives.

The talker's raspy yet high-pitched voice at the other end asked: "Is this Teetlebaum?" I answered calmly, "Yes, this is Rabbi Tattelbaum."

"Have you heard about the Gilstein kidnapping?"

The truth of the matter was that the Gilstein kidnapping had filled the media, newspapers, radio, and television, for days. A teenager was stolen from his affluent suburban home and there was no trail, no hint, and no clue that might solve the crime.

"Yes," I answered, "I've heard about it." His next words chilled my nerve endings and bones because, for reasons I felt only intuitively, he was speaking the truth: "Well," he said, "I am the kidnapper and I want you to be the go-between person between me and the family."

"Why did you call me?" I asked.

"I just picked your name out of the phone book. I want you to call the family and pick up the money and I'll let their son go free. I'll have instructions for you. You see, some time ago Mr. Gilstein did something wrong to me. He hurt me. Now, I will call back later—and *don't call the police.*"

The click of the phone seemed thunderous to me.

I did not follow his orders. I called the local precinct immediately. The on duty officer heard my story. There was a pause. He said, "This is a case for downtown."

I had no idea what "downtown" meant, but soon found out.

Within minutes a call came through from a man who identified himself as the FBI. He explained that a few agents would come by, one by one so as not to arouse suspicion if the caller was watching or monitoring the Temple from somewhere outside.

And so they did come by, one by one at irregular and broad intervals, with their ties loosened and their suit jackets over their arms. All appeared very casual but for one noticeable factor: they all had nicely laundered and pressed white shirts. And they were all impressive-looking, big men with deep voices. They walked into my study flashing their ID shields and giving me their names. I could not help but feel confident with them around me, nor could I keep from noticing the rising panic of the Temple secretary in the outer office.

They asked me to re-cap my brief conversation. One of them had a special mechanism concealed under his coat to connect with my phone line and record whatever was said. They wanted a recording of the caller's voice to play for the family in their home down South and possibly identify the voice.

While we all waited for his next phone call, I called home. I noted a similar tone of panic in my wife's voice when I described the situation to her. She was terribly upset. What if the man, kidnapper or not, knew where we lived and was staking out our apartment building and our children? I tried to reassure her, but my conviction wasn't really strong. When I explained our worry to the FBI special agents, they answered that they would provide their own stakeout of our apartment building. We wouldn't see the agents, but they would be there.

As we waited, the Temple accountant came into the building. I heard him walk up the stairs and, accustomed to his smart-aleck humor, I knew he would say something relevant but irreverent. Sure enough I heard him loud and clear: "Hey, the last time I saw so many white shirts around it was a treasury raid!" His wry sense of humor was a bit lost on the assembled.

Shortly thereafter, the phone rang. It was "the caller." He explained to me again why he wanted to carry out revenge against Mr. Gilstein. He wanted to know if I agreed to help out. I assured him that I would. He said he would call again later to give instructions. Before he hung up, he gave me the Gilsteins' telephone number.

The agent had recorded his voice. It was peculiar that on that particular day there was violent, stormy weather in the southeast. Tornadoes had torn the states of the Southern Atlantic coast in half. Many phone lines were down, but the agents informed me they had "special ways" to get through to the family.

The tape had been rushed downtown. The family heard the caller's voice on the tape. Their reaction was unanimous and immediate: "The voice of the caller to the Rabbi was the voice of the kidnapper!"

From that moment another electronic process began. More agents, suitably casual, wandered into the Temple with equipment concealed on their persons. The wall of the study facing my desk began to fill up. The end result was that from floor to rather high ceiling, the entire wall was filled with complicated electronic equipment to record, to trace, to do whatever might have to be done.

I called my wife on a special line. Keeping her up to date meant driving her into further panic. She was somewhat relieved about the home surveillance but she had every right to be upset. Situations like this had never been covered in the Rabbi's manual or in the seminary's academic curriculum.

If another phone call came through, we were ready. It was time for me to call the Gilstein family on the FBI special hook-up.

I called. A rather hard-sounding voice answered. I offered my name and my heartfelt sympathy. I said I was ready to help. Mr. Gilstein said the family had to be careful. They had already been victims of numerous hoaxes. They would not give out a penny until the kidnapper/ caller answered four questions:

"What did their son Mickey call the station wagon?"

"What did Mickey say to Aunt Hilda every time she called?"

"What color jacket was Mickey wearing?"

"What kinds of knots did the kidnapper use to bind Mickey's hands?"

If the caller could answer these questions, they would proceed further and provide the ransom in cash.

The agents told me that they would not give me any kind of a script. They wanted me to be as loose as possible, to talk as naturally as I was able and not worry about timing. Just talk when the telephone rang.

A very long wait ensued. During that time the agents told me that they were combing their files to find someone who looked like me. They felt that it was dangerous for me to be the "bag man", the go-between who would deliver the $25,000 cash from the family to the kidnapper. They thought they would surely find someone similar in their extensive files.

The telephone finally rang at about 8:00 p.m. I told the caller that I had spoken to the family. "Mr. Gilstein," I said, "sounded wary and skeptical. He posed four questions for you that you would have to answer and not until the answers were satisfactory would they release a penny of the ransom."

As I delivered the questions, I heard a pencil scratching on paper on the other end. I read the questions as slowly as I could without sounding as if I were stalling. At one point I said, "Would you please read that last one back to me?" At that point he must have either suspected a trace or had had enough. He hung up. Within moments it was ascertained that he was calling from somewhere between 59th Street and 14th Street, from 5th Avenue to the East River: data that was essentially hopeless. During the conversation, he did mention something about knives stuck in some of the knots that bound the boy.

It was not till after 11:00 p.m. that he called again. By this time my wife was truly upset. She successfully encouraged me to negotiate with the FBI; until further notice, an FBI car would bring me home that night and take me to and from work for as long as necessary, the "necessary" part remaining open-ended.

I found out a great deal about the FBI during our "waiting periods." Each agent had to be a college graduate. They needed degrees in accounting and rigorous training in detection and criminology. They all seemed caring and dedicated. And they informed me that J. Edgar Hoover had been made aware of my cooperation and sent me his thanks through them.

The late night phone call was extremely brief. It sounded as if the caller was aware of the possibility of a trace. He mentioned a word or two about the color of the jacket and spoke about Aunt Hilda and the station wagon, but without specifics. He said the boy was alive, and then hung up abruptly, as if a sixth sense warned him that the trace was zooming in on him, or as if he was fully apprised of the acute timing necessary for establishing the trace.

He hung up and I never heard from him again. And the entire world never heard from him or from the boy ever again.

Passover that year coincided with Easter so all the school systems in New York City, public, private, parochial and Hebrew after school, were not in session. It had been a harrowing week. My family and I piled into our small station wagon and drove to our minuscule but beloved lakeside cottage in the Connecticut countryside. This time our feeling of escape was decidedly more so, away from the city to this forest-like, utterly rural environment. Our son went out to the front yard to play. We felt a bit of contentment. Our son opened the front door momentarily and said again, "Can I go out to play?" We both gave our immediate consent, because he was already outside playing. After a moment the serenity was broken when my wife said, "It's too quiet out there, let's take a look."

We looked out beyond the front door and around the yard. There was no one there. Irrational panic hit us both. I could not help exclaiming, "O my God, the bastard followed us up to Connecticut!"

Meryl ran to the phone and I ran to the car. No one could have gotten far nor had that much time passed. I drove around the community at breakneck speed. Some of the roads were dirt roads and the tires kicked up a great deal of dust. I cut into the various crossroads. Finally, on the outermost road of the community, there was our son, walking hand in hand with our dear older neighbors who had invited him to go for a walk with them.

I immediately understood the language and intent of a three year old and the extra question: "Can I go out and play?" was really "Can I go out further for a walk?"

My neighbors, who were always delighted by our son's company, seemed perplexed by my reckless driving. I stopped and greeted them as amiably as I could. I forced a huge smile with a warmly expressed "Hi, see you later," and drove back home to calm Meryl down.

There was something very comforting about having FBI protection at home and Temple and commuting to and from work. But within the week it was over. The agents left. The impressive wall of electronic equipment was dismantled and removed (shortly thereafter replaced by dozens of orange crates for the Temple flea market sale). Media attention totally ceased. The mystery, the tragedy, was unresolved until late one afternoon as I was driving home from Sing Sing Prison in Ossining, New York, where a prominent member of our Temple was incarcerated. I visited with him and we had a meaningful talk. He was strong and well spoken, the husband of a woman very active in the Sisterhood, and the father of three young children. He was a forceful man who had been tried and sentenced unforgivingly by a tough judge.

After the visit, on the drive back to Manhattan as I listened to the news, I involuntarily sat bolt upright. The announcer said that Mr. Gilstein had an on-the-air message: "Would the kidnapper please, please call the New York City Rabbi again! They would like him to communicate with the Rabbi." The "hardness" may have left Gilstein's voice as he pleaded for a response, but to my dying day I will never understand why Mr. Gilstein or the family did not alert me about the public plea.

When I reached home I immediately called the special agent in charge of the kidnapping case who had left me his number. He said he could not understand the matter himself, especially since he and other authorities had strongly advised the family not to make the plea at all. But ultimately there were no further phone calls from the caller or the family.

I told only a few people about my involvement in the case.

For a number of years I received newspaper clippings from family and friends that Mickey had been sighted in places from Oklahoma to Israel.

No lead ever truly surfaced. The kidnapping has remained an unsolved, tragic mystery. I did receive a letter of commendation from J. Edgar Hoover.

No "messenger" stayed Abraham's hand from the altar of sacrifice, as in the Book of Genesis. Unlike the bound Isaac, son of Abraham, Mickey's redemption never came.

Conning an Ex-Con

I WAS truly eager to begin my work as the Rabbi of the "Village Temple," the official name of which is still Congregation B'nai Israel of Greenwich Village. My two-year contract stipulated that I was to begin my position on the miserably hot day of August 15, 1965.

I had just left a three-year assistantship at a large Upper East Side congregation. Three years as an assistant was helpful but truly quite enough for me. In spite of the fact that I had a "difference" of thought, philosophy and goal with the leadership of the big synagogue, I basically kept these "differences" to myself. As an Assistant Rabbi, ultimate action should be guided by loyalty; one is there to learn, follow, accommodate, and be helpful in every way possible. But those three years of assistantship helped me define what I really wanted to be and to represent.

Anthropomorphism seemed to be the normal mode of prayer book theological address. I was tired of the stuffy, old, regular prayer book. I never really believed in a personal God involved in human history. The Holocaust, personal family tragedy, as well as healthy doubts of all people who take the spiritual side of life seriously had long ago demolished a "traditional" notion of God.

I felt liberated by deeper understandings of traditional texts:

> Abraham: "Shall not the Judge of all the earth do justly."
> Genesis
> Moses: "Who shall I say sent me?" ... "I shall be what I shall be!"
>
> Exodus

Moses: *"Show me your essence!"* ... *"No one can see me
and yet still live."*

Exodus

And liberated as well by the philosophical wrestlings of so many of
my ancestors whose souls were tortured by the fundamentalist notions
of a person-like God.

I was deeply comforted by the Book of Job, the observations of Philo,
the theological radicalism of Moses Maimonides and to a limited extent
by Spinoza (so foolishly excommunicated by an insecure post-Spanish-
expulsion Dutch Jewish community), the teachings of Mordecai
Kaplan, and a small collection of post-Holocaust theologians including
Elie Wiesel, Richard Rubenstein, and Emil Fackenheim, among many
others).

Yes, there is the world of ideas, ideals, theological challenges and
creative manipulation of vast Jewish literary sources into the Sabbath
Festival, and High Holy Day liturgies. But first there are the people,
the people who founded and maintain and help run the congregation's
affairs, people who truly believe that the congregation is theirs, as well
as the Rabbi's.

When I served as Navy Chaplain assigned to the U.S. Marines
at Parris Island, I felt it was necessary to wear a simple soft kippah
or yarmulke (skullcap) on my head. The Jewish troops came from a
multitude of backgrounds. Wearing a skullcap was the "norm" for most
of them. I was perfectly comfortable wearing one while I conducted
services. I was truly more at ease with one than without.

When I emerged from military service and served at the large Upper
East Side Temple, a synagogue founded before there was a "reform"
movement, the norm was also that a head covering be worn. However,
the mode was different. Both Rabbi and Cantor wore the high biretta
style of head covering. I hated it. I wore a simple flat cloth skullcap.
Some of the concerned ladies of the Sisterhood told the Senior Rabbi
that they would buy a biretta for me. The Senior Rabbi, in his wisdom
and understanding, said to them, "It's all right—let him alone."

When I came to the Village Temple and was engaged as the Rabbi,
having "passed" all the tests of "normalcy" and "theology", we utterly
forgot to talk about pulpit ritual. When I told a few trustees of my plan
to wear a simple skullcap there was general consternation about my

declaration. This had never been done before at the Village Temple. It became an issue. It is said that Rabbi Stephen Wise once declared that if the Reform Movement had not removed the yarmulke there never would have been a Conservative Movement in Jewish life. Possibly so. For far too many Jews it was a "hot button" issue.

The issue was raised and confronted. In view of the fact that there was "freedom of the pew" in this regard, there could also be "freedom of the pulpit." A stormy congregational meeting was avoided.

But that issue was the very least of my initial problems.

I will never forget the angst of my first real human predicament.

Just before I came to the Village Temple, its previous president was put in jail. It was a "white collar crime" and the man had a wife and three young children. The judge who sentenced him was known as a "hanging judge" and took no notice of his or his lawyer's plea for mercy. His defense lawyer was also a member of the Temple's Board of Trustees and Chairperson of the Search Committee that had selected me.

Factions of the congregation were up in arms. The former president served his full prison term. He was scheduled for release just before the High Holy Days. It was the tradition of the Temple to honor its past presidents by having them hold the Torah during the emotional singing of the Kol Nidrei on the evening of Yom Kippur. Those holding the Torah were a symbolic righteous tribunal of Yom Kippur judgment!

Dozens of calls came to me at the office and every night at home exclaiming that such an honor should not be given to a convicted criminal just out of jail. Trusting in the goodness and reasonableness of human nature, I felt that a good and sincere heart-to-heart talk with the past president would resolve the problem. My hope was that after a talk with me, he would graciously withdraw and not be the source of any harmful dissension in the Temple.

I think I learned more about the vagaries of perverse human nature and Temple politics in that half hour over coffee than in three years as an Assistant Rabbi. He would have none of my request. He had served his time. Justice had been done and he would steadfastly, courageously assert his right and privilege, as was his entitlement in keeping with the long-standing, venerable tradition of the Temple. He would not be denied the honor of holding a Torah during Kol Nidrei.

In addition to his "in-your-face" refusal, he contacted at least a dozen of the Trustees of the Board and members-at-large to call me and berate me for my sycophantic (his term, not mine!) injustice.

By the time I received the sixteenth late-night call, I was an emotional wreck.

I made my decision. I knew what I felt had to be done. I knew what I had to do.

Rosh Hashanah went well. I felt that I had put my special personal mark upon the life of the congregation. After my strong insistence, the congregation abolished the selling of tickets for the High Holy Days, and like most congregations, required membership. It worked! Those who were in my corner could claim with me that the membership of the Temple had nearly doubled in size, within the time frame of only a bit more than one month.

Rosh Hashanah, with all its electrifying drama, came and went. Kol Nidrei and Yom Kippur were dead ahead.

When we got to the Kol Nidrei service, I announced that we would follow the "tradition" of nearly utter darkness in the sanctuary so that each person could be truly alone with one's deepest inner thoughts and feelings and memories. I had done this with the U.S. Marines while serving as a Navy Chaplain at Parris Island because I wanted to avoid the glaring fluorescent lights.

After the lights were extinguished, I called the Torah holders forth without calling names. No one could really see them. If it was an honor (which it was), it was veiled in a lovely, heavy pervading darkness. The congregation could barely see the pulpit. The Cantor could barely see his musical notes. Those on the pulpit could barely see the congregants.

The Torahs were lifted and held. The Kol Nidrei was beautifully chanted. I think I have never heard it sung with such meaning and sweetness.

In order to extend the exalted feeling, I had the quiet darkness linger till after the scrolls were replaced in the Ark and the holders had been seated.

The darkness covered the controversy.

A feeling of relief and satisfaction permeated the sanctuary—our "jewel of a shul!"

A lot of people gave me wordless "thumbs up" after the service was over.

The House that Apricot Danish Built

WE had happily bought a tiny country house in rural western Connecticut, near the shore of a lovely, large lake. The house, or cottage, measured 20 feet by 36 feet, exactly standard for 4x8 foot wallboard inside and plywood outside. We loved the place but had no money, no desire to move and a growing family.

A solution came to us: expand the house with the labor of my own hands. There wasn't much time in which to do it. Free weekends were non-existent as I was the only rabbi of the Village Temple. Vacation time was always interrupted. Money was also a factor. It wasn't there.

I had borrowed a "how-to-expand-your-house" book from the local library. Miraculously, it portrayed an expansion amazingly similar to the vision of remodeling we had in our minds. We would break out the outside wall of the living room and enlarge the room, and add on a large playroom to serve as an all-in-one guestroom/utility room/ workshop. I renewed the book by phone every two weeks from the accommodating town library, to the extent that I actually had it checked out for two years.

At that time the money factor—or lack of it—was crucial. But then, quite unexpectedly, the money came from a surprising source.

It was known to nearly everyone in the Village that New York University had amassed huge resources in order to buy up enormous properties for its downtown campus. Rumor had it that one of the reasons for this campaign was to avoid a situation similar to that of Columbia University way uptown on Morningside Heights, a university campus surrounded by declining slums, poverty and crime, a factor experienced by other urban campuses as well.

The purchasing program was enormously effective. Hundreds of millions of dollars were spent buying, renovating, and reconstructing apartment houses, warehouses, garages, townhouses, and all kinds of residential and commercial properties.

One such acquisition was an apartment house on lower Fifth Avenue to be reconfigured as a dormitory. After much legal wrangling all but one of the tenants were removed. That tenant was a lovely elderly lady well within her eighth decade of life. She would not move. She could not be compelled or compensated. So the university in its wisdom co-opted her. She remained in her tiny apartment and was listed as a "dormitory mother. She was Italian-Jewish, from a family of "Sephardic Italian" descent, and her name reflected both heritages: Frayda Fratello.

This was a family name well known in New York City, a name that graced a chain of produce stores all over Manhattan. They enjoyed a fine reputation for top quality goods. One paid a slightly higher price, but one went to Fratello's for fresh, high level merchandise.

Over the years the stores of the chain were phased out, bought out and pushed out. But to many the name brought images of honesty and high quality.

Frayda Fratello's "dormitory home" was near the Village Temple. She told us that officially she and members of her extended family were long-time members of the huge Temple Emanu-El uptown. However, since she lived near the Village Temple and enjoyed its intimacy and cheeriness, she began to attend services regularly.

There was something very lovely about her. She had pure silver hair bound tightly into a bun in the back, iridescent blue eyes, and she was neat and comely, a tidy small sparkling package always clad in clean, white sneakers. She had a beautiful smile and smiled often.

She became a fixture of our Friday evening Shabbat services. Whether she officially became a member of the Temple or not was irrelevant. She was a faithful, reverent, scintillating presence in our Temple, and it seemed that everyone knew and respected her personal victory against the mighty New York University real estate development program.

Many of the members had fought some of the University's acquisitions and zoning changes all the way to the Supreme Court—

and lost. The legal battles filled The New York Times for years on end. Once the final decisions were rendered, the community acknowledged defeat, patted itself on the back for a courageous try, and accepted the new libraries, student centers, research halls and living quarters. They accepted defeat, but revered the little elderly lady who had "won" her own personal battle.

One Friday evening, I was informed after services that Ms. Fratello had left a package for my wife and me. The aftermath of services on a Friday night, as at most Temples with a late service, was quite hectic. We paid no attention to the package until we got home.

Carefully wrapped inside a box was an apricot Danish ring from the now-vanished Schraffts, once famous for its pastries, ice cream, and teatime fare.

We dived into it and washed it down with cold milk. The taste was special, memorable, but the source of the gift even more so.

Apricot Danish after apricot Danish appeared on Friday nights for almost two years. It was a wonderful ritual that enhanced our Friday nights—even in later memory.

Suddenly the Danish offerings stopped and Frayda Fratello was not to be found in Temple on Friday nights.

I called wherever I could, the dorm, other Fratellos, until finally I found a relative who informed me that she was terribly ill and in New York University Hospital. I rushed to be by her side. Even ill, bedridden, she had an aura of spiritual beauty. I could not help but remark to her about her beautiful blue eyes that looked up from the pillow; eyes surrounded by sweet smile lines.

Frayda recovered, left the hospital and returned home. She resumed her attendance at the Friday night services and the apricot Danish rings reappeared.

Summertime came. I took my family on vacation, this time for an uninterrupted few weeks. When we returned to the city, there was no Frayda, no apricot Danish rings, no beautiful blue-eyed spirituality.

What I found was a lawyer's letter. It contained her will. She had died. I was heartsick that I did not know that she had died, and my wife was as sad as I.

We read the will. She had left a fortune in legacies: to hospitals, temples, Jewish cultural centers, and lovely personal bequests to nearly everyone who had touched her life. Though nostalgic and saddened, I was proud and thrilled to be among them.

There it was, the money we needed to fulfill the vision of enlarging our country place. After the passage of numerous years, the playroom we called the "Fratello Wing" became the "Fratello Study" and it is in tribute to her memory and caring that I am so happy to study and write there and occasionally recall the tangy and sweet freshness of the apricot Danish ring.

An apricot Danish ring will always be similar in effect to the recollection aroused by Marcel Proust's biscuit. The tang and taste evoke a world of nostalgic loving remembrance.

Who Was Vito Tamari?

OUR rabbinic class was ordained in 1960 at a time when there was a military draft. Members of the clergy were exempt from the draft, or so some of us thought. But we were essentially "drafted" into the military by our own rabbinic organization, The Central Conference of American Rabbis. The concept behind the "conscription" was simple: if you chose not to serve a two-year stint as a military chaplain, the Placement Commission would not place you in a congregation. Some of my colleagues had already served in the armed forces and were not required to serve again but most of us "volunteered." Each was given the right to choose a branch of military service. Some went Army, some went Air Force, and some went Navy. I had always liked boats and was partial to the navy blue dark uniform. I chose the Navy.

In 1960, I was ordained on June 6, married on June 12, and reported to duty on June 14 at the Navy Chaplains' Indoctrination program at U.S. Naval Base, Newport, Rhode Island. Before and during preparation for service to the Navy, I felt it was important to hone rabbinic and ritual skills with the understanding that I could be sent anywhere in the world and would have to rely only on my own mettle for skilled ritual expression. So I taught myself to blow the shofar. As is generally known, this is not easy. The horn itself is fashioned in a specific ancient traditional way. Some are large, some very large, and some are small. In order to blow the shofar properly and in a kosher, acceptable manner, one cannot use a mouthpiece or any other aid foreign to the horn of a ram (or a relative of similar species).

The Jewish Welfare Board, the organization that is an invaluable support system for all Jewish chaplains the world over, sent me a small Shofar. I practiced on it day and night. It had a shrill, high sound. I became capable of blowing all the required calls and signals after months of practice.

This skill was to prove quite useful down through the years, especially during my Village days.

The wife of our cantor produced a highly popular television program, and her husband's profession was well known in television circles. She was asked if he would blow the shofar at a studio recording of an album for a movie musical. He responded that he was unable to blow the shofar but would ask his Rabbi about doing so.

When asked, I was intrigued and quite willing. The $96.00 that I would be paid on Actor's Equity scale was of no matter—I was curious, and I showed up promptly at the recording studio on 42nd Street. I had no knowledge of the show either, the highly successful Broadway musical "Godspell." Though I had heard of it, I knew nothing of its content. Everything I was called upon to do with the shofar was totally "out of context." "Would you please blow a long, high F sharp?" "Would you kindly give a short C note?" "Would you repeat this and that and hold the note for as long as you can?" "Would you interrupt with various staccato blasts?"

I did not have technical musical knowledge; I knew the proper ritual calls and could play them. If I was in proper practice and smooth of lip and breath, I could even, from time to time, haltingly play the opening notes of "My Country 'tis of Thee"! But I was scarcely a seasoned pro.

I blew, and the musicians and technicians agreed it was "high F," "low C," etc. in proper frequency and length. I was lauded and cheered. I had done my bit for American popular culture but I had not investigated the production itself.

I discovered that "Godspell" was a symbolic rock presentation of the life of Jesus and his disciples. At the beginning of the play, soon to be a movie, a shofar call would summon the "modern apostles" to the "Passion of Jesus".

I preferred *not* to have my name appear on the record jacket, so I needed a pseudonym. My Hebrew name is Chayyim, which means "life." Roughly translated to Italianate Latin, my first name became "Vito." Tattelbaum means "tree of dates" or simply palm tree, which in Hebrew is "tamar." Put them together with a slight Romanesque flourish, and we have: "Shofar—blown by Vito Tamari."

That's the way the album was published, and if you should find an old 33 rpm collector's item of "Godspell The Movie Album" at a tag sale somewhere, that's the way it remained!

Uncommon Weddings
I Have Known

Wedding I

WHEREVER one serves as a rabbi in Manhattan, be it uptown or downtown, one is likely to officiate at a wedding at a certain world-famous Hotel. Both before and after its renovation it epitomizes elegance: from the bronze-gated elevators to the marble floors, the gilded walls, the flowing drapes, the haute cuisine service and fare, and the old world ambience.

It was all there at a late Saturday night wedding: tuxes, tails and gowns, a full white bridal gown, a score of men and women as ushers and bridesmaids, a classical quartet for processional musical background, and changing lighting for the various stages of the ceremony. When the procession to the chupa ended, the videotaping and candid flash photography ceased. I began the ceremony.

All went well until suddenly a huge brown water bug/cockroach jumped up on the lower part of the front of the bride's gown. No one in the assemblage saw it, except the bride, the groom, the best man, the maid of honor, the two sets of parents, and the Rabbi and Cantor.

It proceeded to climb up the gown, higher and higher. Except for the panic of the bride and her low moaning, there was utter silence. Attention to the words of my ceremony was rapt. I noticed the Cantor's chanting weakening a bit. Decisive action was called for!

I stopped speaking. The creature was almost waist high. I put my Rabbi's manual in my left hand. My right hand was now free.

I struck.

I swiped my hand down the front of the gown—the monster fell to the floor.

I struck again with my right foot as quickly and as hard as I could.

Those of us at the chupa heard the crunch while those who were in the congregation and not paying close attention heard the loud stamp of a foot. Thinking it was the groom breaking the glass at the end of the ceremony, they applauded and loudly proclaimed, "Mazal Tov!"

The bride was enormously relieved, the groom grateful. Sighs of satisfaction came from those around me. Many in the audience were confused as the Cantor and I calmly continued the ceremony until it was over, to be climaxed yet again by the groom's breaking of the glass.

As I left the pulpit, I couldn't help but notice one big, dead upside-down roach on the floor. It too had paid the price for an elegant wedding.

Later, during cocktails, I overheard a comment: "I guess that's the way it is now with modern ceremonies, even the Rabbi breaks a glass."

Wedding II

IT'S AN old but risky custom for both bride and groom to fast the day of the wedding until the wedding feast.

Sometimes the fast is begun, but not fully completed. Such was the case before the ceremony when both bride and groom who had fasted were enticed by friends to drink some wine, possibly champagne, before the ceremony.

The wine rendered the bride very shaky. The groom, a big muscular football star, seemed to handle the unwise imbibing rather well.

The ceremony began.

The various participants in the procession proceeded in their turns down the aisle. I noted a troubled look on the faces of some, my first indication that something awkward was brewing near the starting area of the procession. It was the bride. All eyes were upon her. She was shaken. Her steps were uneven. She was turning pale and perspiring. I was sure that she would not make it to her place under the chupah. She progressed slowly. Escorted by her dad, she got as far as the front row. The groom came out to take her. She exchanged kisses with her father. She moved shakily but lightly to the arm of the groom. A fleeting moment of recognition passed between them. He led her forward. Up one step, then the next. She made it. They were standing in front of me beneath the chupah.

At that moment, the groom fainted.

The best man, the Cantor and I caught him just in time. Everyone in the room seemed to break into panic at the same moment. We led him to a chair beside the ark. We pushed his head down between his knees; the blood flow to the brain was re-established. He was green but came out of it. He shook his head, cleared the cobwebs, straightened his bow tie, and took his place beside the bride. His sheepish look endured throughout the rest of the ceremony, which proceeded to completion without interruption.

I really meant it when I said "mazal tov" after the groom broke the glass.

Wedding III

I'M SURE it's happened to other Rabbis. I usually check out the details carefully before every ceremony. But, Pedro, the perfect Temple custodian, had set everything up for a wedding ceremony in the "jewel of a schul"—the sanctuary of the Village Temple – or so I thought.

The Cantor sang; the procession began. All parties were placed properly beneath the chupah. Anticipation and satisfaction seemed to be universally shared until I (and no one else) realized there was no cup of wine for the ceremony.

The closest container of wine was a walk to the rear of the sanctuary, through the door in the lobby, a left turn and up a steep flight of stairs, all the way through the entire length of the social hall to the kitchen and the refrigerator in its farthest corner.

It couldn't be done.

I continued the ceremony. At a certain point beyond the exchange of vows, I called for eyes to be closed in mystic, spiritual hope and for the silence of the unuttered prayers of the heart. In that moment, I glided silently to the organ room on my left. The organ sat there and on its lid, a small Dixie cup with water that had to be at least three days old. I hadn't the power to turn water into wine, as did other religious innovators at other times, but I did have the power to deceive. It was too late to manipulate the Cantor to the proper blessing, so the blessing over wine was sung; the water was drunk twice, as is the custom, and the ceremony smoothly done as thought all, except me. In my heart I blessed Johnny Watkins, our organist, for being both thirsty *and* negligent, a combination that enabled me to manipulate the circumstances into a successful ceremony.

Although I am a confirmed rationalist (with some mystical, poetic lapses) I always wondered if that particular deception contributed to the divorce of that couple years later.

Intermission: A Wedding Aside

I'VE CONDUCTED weddings in many places in Manhattan: The Rose Garden in Central Park just before a torrential rainstorm; on the QE2 docked in harbor; on a dining cruise ship; in a convent (with all crosses covered by bed sheets); in front of a raging fireplace bonfire that burned the seat of my trousers; in countless living rooms, hospital rooms, ballrooms, classrooms, sick rooms, rooftop terraces, UN chapels, storefront tents, zoos, botanical gardens, glens, hills, penthouses, basements—and of course, synagogues, sanctuaries and chapels.

I've gone the gamut from grooms or brides who have said "Make it short"; "Make it long"; "Make it tasteful, there will be gentiles present"; "Don't mention God"; "Make God permeate the room"; "Don't use Hebrew"; "Don't use the English vows"; "Just proclaim our marriage and say nothing else"; "Use every ancient traditional phrase and ritual you can"; "Of course, you'll stay for dinner"; "Of course, you will be leaving"; "We want a Cantor to officiate with you"; "We don't want a Cantor involved."

One sprightly little Orthodox Rabbi stepped up to co-officiate on the pulpit with me. He asked very seriously, "Will the Cantor be here?"

When I told him "No," he said, "Good, thank God, they make me deaf!"

Wedding IV

MURRAY CALLED. "Rabbi, my wife is dying here at home. Our daughter is going to be married. Can we do the ceremony in her bedroom?"

Murray was a storekeeper. He always rented large spaces and would sell at a profit anything he could get his hands on, from boxes of barrettes to key chains, whistles, balloons, baking and kitchen utensils, paper goods, clothing seconds, flags of all nations and slogans, t-shirts of every industry, corporation, celebrity or sports team. If you didn't need it, he had it. And he had it in huge quantities. It was fun to enter his store located just above the boundary line of the Village. He and his family had lived in the Village for decades and he and his wife often came to services.

He was not poor. He was the "odd-lot jobber" extraordinaire. He was Price-Costco before there was Price-Costco; he was Sam's long before Wal-Mart took over much of the world; he was "Christmas Tree Shops" before discounting on "chatchkas" was even invented. He did all right but was not a retailing magnate.

In an offbeat way, I became responsible for his leap to enormous success.

Not far from my apartment building, a small store was established in a low-rise building that no longer exists. Below the store's name was a small sign whose quotation struck me happily: "Cheerful things for Sale." As a Seminary professor said to our rabbinical class long ago, "Everything is grist for the sermonic mill."

In spite of all the pain, the dispossession, the disenfranchisements, the persecutions, the tragedy and wanderings of the Jewish people, a vast majority of Jews always chose to remain Jews. In spite of upheaval and agony, the blessings were chanted, the lines of liturgy cantillated, the songs of the festivals sung. It was not only a response to terrible challenges or a deep inner rejection of outside practices and impossible theologies. Within the heart of Judaism and the observances of the Jewish people, there was also joy. The underlying theme was sounded through the centuries, despite whatever pain, that life is a gift to be cherished, nurtured, ceremonialized, expressed, sung, a gift of exultation and exaltation, of triumph over the abyss of sorrow. The one hundredth Psalm proclaims:

Ivdu et Adonai besimcha, Worship the Eternal in joy
Bo-u lefanav birnana, Come before God with song.

All this paean of joy was the background of an enthusiastic Friday night Shabbat sermon, a reaction to and inclusion of the quotation from the store: "Cheerful things for sale!"

Murray and his wife listened carefully. The thought struck them like lightning on a dark summer's night. That was the essence of their store.

When they asked my permission to use the phrase, I told them that I could not withhold that which was not mine. The phrase was not franchised or patented or copyrighted. It came from the land of free speech.

They used it. They put a large sign in the window of their store. Business boomed. Goods poured in and moved out quickly at a profit. The phrase caught the fancy of the many people who crowded the streets near the store. It was no longer a store that sold assorted junk and chatchkas, it was now an emporium that had cheerful things for sale for every strand of humanity.

Murray became a rich man, rich beyond his most ardent ambitions. Within a short span of years he sold the business and prepared to move to Florida.

It was then that Pearl took sick. All thought of moving was on hold. He had nurses around the clock to tend to Pearl at home.

His daughter's forthcoming marriage seemed to give him little joy. He referred to his future son-in-law as "that crazy hop-head!"

When I met with the engaged couple I could see why. Beside some totally irrational hostility, the prospective groom had strict instructions for me regarding the wedding ceremony. There was to be no ritual, no quotations, no blessings, only that I was to proclaim in one sentence that he and his wife were married. Murray's daughter seemed as fervent about this as her husband-to-be.

For the sake of Murray and Pearl, I was patience personified—but I stood my ground as a Rabbi. I could not simply proclaim their marriage. The ceremony could be surprisingly short, but if I, or any other Rabbi, were going to officiate, certain elements of the ancient ceremony of Jewish marriage had to be included. The discussion, in spite of my forbearance, became heated. They knew of Murray and Pearl's attachment to me and of their caring and loyalty. I promised they would not be made unhappy or uncomfortable by my conducting of the ceremony. None of us anticipated a wedding ceremony in the bedroom of a dying mother. Though great sadness attended the ritual, that sadness of setting made everything much easier than I had anticipated.

They were married and had children. They were divorced and went far away from each other.

Pearl died.

I think I officiated at Murray's next two or three marriages.

Wedding V

THE WEDDING was scheduled to take place in one of those lovely, private, Italianate mansions on Park Avenue in the 60s. I believe that part of the Rockefeller family had once lived there. One could rent the premises for festive purposes.

I had my extensive premarital discussions with the bride and groom and all details had been covered; everything should have been in readiness. For a number of years, I brought a portable chupah with me for wedding ceremonies. But in later years, the number of commitments for any particular day made matters too complicated to do that. A rented chupah for ceremonies had been ordered from a Jewish book and ritual store many times before, quite successfully, until the day of the wedding at the Rockefeller mansion.

Everything and everyone was there, except the chupah! I called the store. It had been sent out a long time ago and it never came back. And it was impossible that Sunday to contract for a new one.

The missing chupah caused grief. But it was early. Something could be done.

I had my large tallit. I told the maintenance man of the building to gather every broom or broom-like instrument that he could. After a few minutes he reappeared with two long plastic brooms, one wooden one, and a plunger. With the aid of elastic bands, I was able to knot two corners of the tallit to the top of the broom handles. The sweeping parts thankfully screwed off. The brush on the wooden one, however, was not removable. The custodian brought me a long tomato knife with a serrated edge. I sawed and sawed until the straw sweeper was removed, banged a nail in the top but was then stymied for the fourth pole. I simply could not use a plunger rod for a wedding ceremony!

The man finally found another forlorn old broom. I proceeded to saw off the handle. I screwed an eyelet into the top, connected the four corners of the tallit as a canopy and behold! A chupah, a ceremony, a wedding!

The blisters on my hand bothered me for only a few days of the following week.

Wedding VI

IT WAS a fall wedding. The weather was beautifully autumnal, cool and pleasant, but the days were getting shorter and shorter.

If a couple wanted to schedule their ceremony for Saturday night, which many do, I would not be a stickler concerning the exact timing for the end of Shabbat. I felt that it was overly burdensome to wait for the traditional "three stars" to be seen in the sky signaling the beginning of the next day. As long as the sun was setting and shadows began to abound, I would officiate.

One couple, with whom I remain friendly and loving till this day, arranged to have their wedding ceremony and reception at a truly beautiful, soul-filling spot high up overlooking the Hudson River just north of Manhattan.

The out-of-doors setting was superb. We felt as if the shadows of the beautiful sunset west across the river were embracing us. I began the ceremony. Suddenly, all in the space of one moment, the sunset turned into absolute darkness. I could barely see the faces of the bride and groom. The general direction of my sight was assisted by the whiteness of the bridal gown whose outline I could just barely discern. The assembled congregation, only a few yards away, disappeared into the blackness. Worst of all, *I could not see my manual.*

This had never happened before. In literally thousands of ceremonies, I had never found myself in total darkness. But the thousands before helped. I did not realize how deeply and permanently the ceremony was imprinted on my cerebellum. Carrying out and reciting the rites from sheer memory was scary, but doable. A remark I then made citing the difficulty and the brazen courage needed to overcome it helped loosen the tension. I was astonished myself on how little need I had of the printed words. The ceremony proceeded without pause or interruption or loss of place nearly until the end. When it was almost over, there was a momentary delay when the groom had to search for the glass in order to break it.

On a Rainy Day

THE past weekend had been brutally busy. After a hugely successful Friday night service, a Shabbat morning service with an enormous Bat Mitzvah followed, then some major programming on Sunday morning and work all afternoon Sunday with counseling and lifecycle ceremonies,

Monday came, and with Monday morning came the enormous physical gloom of unrelenting torrential rains. It was a good day to relax, unwind, lie down, read a book. The book that day was Herman Wouk's "Youngblood Hawke", a somewhat disguised fictional biography of Thomas Wolfe. Many authors' writings have been a source of joy and profundity, from Dostoyevsky to Schwartz-Bart, but I always loved the mechanical precision of Wouk and the free-flowing outpouring of emotion of Thomas Wolfe. As the day moved on, the rains got heavier and I was immersed in the book.

I am a rationalist. I don't believe in "Fingers of God" or the hand of God in human history. If you ask me to define what I think or believe, I fall back on a kind of poetic mysticism. There is something, I don't know what. Is there a metaphysical something beyond the physical universe? The metaphysical something lies within us, within heart and intellect. Sometimes one can feel the profound spirituality of existence but more often the indefinable despair of being.

Wouk's deeply touching scene of Youngblood Hawke's death reached into me, and it was as if a metaphysical hand plucked a heartstring inside. Almost mechanically, as if driven by a force outside me, I got up, put on my raingear, called the garage for my car, and was soon on my way along the East River Drive headed downtown.

Sylvan Defleur was considered "the intellectual" on the Board of

Trustees of the Village Temple. He was extremely well read, highly educated, loved to converse with intelligence and depth, and wrote very well. He wrote reviews of musical and theatrical performances for local downtown newspapers, and his name and reputation were well known in the Village. He was married to Esther, an infinitely sweet woman, who was a talented concert pianist. They were a most unusual couple.

Their only fault was that they could hardly scratch out a living. They were always neat but threadbare, kind and sensitive but nearly starving intellectuals. If they had not lived in a tiny, radically rent-controlled apartment on a small, obscure street in Greenwich Village, they might have been homeless. Other trustees told me that, on occasion, they had helped them pay the rent and buy groceries. Years later I was proud to learn that I was chosen for the position of Rabbi because I passed the intellectual requirements laid down by Sylvan Defleur.

After a few years, Sylvan fell upon hard times when he suffered a physical decline. His speech became slurred, his appetite disappeared, and his gait was shaky. The diagnosis was a tumor in the brain. Surgery was attempted but proved to be of only short-lasting value. His condition deteriorated. It was too much for Esther to handle by herself.

The only logical place for him to find the proper care was at St. Rosa's Hospital just by the East River, a hospice administered and staffed by nuns. It was beautifully maintained and the nursing care of the nuns was impeccable. The roster of patients included the impoverished of the city but the care they received was better than anyone's resources could buy.

Filled with a sense of urgent compassion aroused by Herman Wouk's description of Youngblood Hawke's death, I drove down to St. Rosa's in the rain. There was no choice in this for me. I had to do it.

I had visited Sylvan numerous times before—but this rainy day was now not my own.

He sat up in bed. The scar on his head was deep. He was weak, but he was articulate.

"No human being should have to endure this." I held his hand as we talked. I was able to distract him from his discomfort ever so slightly. We talked and then sat in silence for nearly an hour. The sisters began to hint that it was time to go. Even though he was not eating, they always tried to feed him. I embraced him and left.

I drove slowly north on the East River Drive. It was rush hour then and fortunately traffic moved very slowly, fortunately because the East River is a constantly changing, evanescing, exciting, beautiful scene. In heavy rains the Drive always fills with water, but I was in no rush.

When I got home, I felt relieved. The sense of urgency was gone.

That night, some time in the early dark before dawn, Esther called. Sylvan had died, only a few moments earlier.

In spite of the sadness, something deep within was witness to a new mystic linkage in my life. I felt a certain physical tension and sorrow that was not unpleasant, a sense of the moving thrill and constancy of birth, life, and death. Sometimes the infinite has meaning.

"Religious Emphasis Week"

(There Was "Emphasis", All Right, But I'm Not Sure How "Religious" It Was)

I RECEIVED a phone call from the Chancellor of the Jewish Chautauqua Society (an organization affiliated with the former Union of American Hebrew Congregations, now the Union for Reform Judaism). The Society's main agenda was to organize Christian-Jewish meetings, lectures and conferences on college campuses and its success in these matters has been far-reaching.

Would Mrs. Tattelbaum (Meryl) and I be the central focus of "Religious Emphasis Week" sponsored by two upstate New York colleges located in the same town? We would.

With babysitters properly in place, off we went. We were to stay with the local Protestant college chaplain, his wife and daughter in their large, rambling picturesque dwelling.

The minister was a tall, slim attractive man. He had a way of speaking in conversation that enveloped me. I didn't dare be inattentive to anything he said. His wife was a comely, dark-haired, olive-skinned beauty. Their daughter was ethereal in her tall, slim attractiveness. She informed us that she would be going away, to a friend's house, for a few days.

As we were given a tour of the house, Meryl and I could not help but notice a very obviously displayed copy of the recently published book "Open Marriage" on the desk in the minister's study.

On the first evening of our arrival, we were joined by another young minister and his wife. He served as assistant pastor at a large church in town.

During dinner, the four of them informed us they had just returned from a refreshing swim, followed by a nude sauna. We expressed mild surprise, but were told this was a common occurrence.

Dinner was early. I was scheduled to lead a teaching session at the college that evening. I found the college session tumultuous, as if an entire roomful of students was waiting in ambush. The charge was led by a young woman who, after dissecting one of my statements about interfaith marriage, informed me she had become a "Jew for Jesus." My reaction to this apostasy was strong and evoked equally strong reactions. It was not a pleasant session and it left me ill at ease.

At the end of this session we bade farewell to the local minister and his wife and went back home with the chaplain and his spouse.

The chaplain suggested that we all get comfortable, change into our pajamas and robes and re-gather in the living room. Meryl and I were young. We wanted to be accommodating guests. We followed his suggestion and reported back to the living room in comfortable attire.

There were candles burning and the room was filled with the aroma of incense. The minister was dressed in a striking robe, looking like a very young Charlton Heston in the days when Heston played Moses, but without the staff. The young minister's beard was red. His wife looked svelte and comfortable.

They initiated little peaceful rituals of friendship in which individually we would talk to each other, touch one another, and wish each other peace and blessing.

During this exotic "get-acquainted" there was no question in my mind that he was looking hard at Meryl and seemed to lean forward constantly in her direction.

Meryl and I felt very uncomfortable. Without saying anything, we felt that we knew where this whole scene was heading.

At the earliest moment that we could, we said goodnight.

When we got to the bedroom, we looked at each other anxiously. We were utterly quiet. We waited. We heard footsteps rising on the stairs, very slow footsteps. They stopped outside our door for a few moments that seemed endless. Then the footsteps resumed and we discerned at last that they were going away. We clung to each other in child-like panic. The footsteps moved off into another direction, away from our door.

We both slept fitfully that night.

The morning after, the minister was cold and remote.

Years later, we learned that they had moved to another far away college assignment and that their marriage had ended in divorce.

If theirs was an "open" marriage, was mine a "closed" one?

A Holocaust of One

NEARLY everyone knows the story, but for me it began in a very personal way.

Years ago, a middle-aged woman in elegant dress and coiffure came to my study at the Village Temple, to interview me. She lived nearby, had two young daughters and wanted to enroll them in Hebrew school for a Jewish education. The family joined the Village Temple and became devoted members and students. The Klinghoffer family and I retained our warm contacts throughout the years, even after I had moved to the position of Senior Rabbi at another temple uptown. It was my pleasure to have officiated at their daughters' ceremonies of Bat Mitzvah, Confirmation, and to have been the rabbi who conducted both of their weddings and the naming of their sons.

One wedding, Lisa's, took place long before the tragedy, the other, Ilsa's, shortly after it.

The tragedy of their parents is known all over the world.

The Klinghoffers wanted to celebrate their 36th wedding anniversary by taking a Mediterranean cruise together with a large group of friends. They flew to Italy and boarded the Italian luxury cruise liner the Achille Lauro.

Leon Klinghoffer was in failing health and at age 69 was wheelchair bound. It was not known at the time publicly, but Marilyn Klinghoffer had already contracted colon cancer, which had spread. The cruise was to have been a high point of their lives.

The ship had left Italy and was docked in Egypt. The land call after Egypt was to have been Ashdod, one of the port cities of Israel.

When they returned from sightseeing early in the day, they found a film crew shooting a movie scene at the foot of the gangplank. The set was noisy and chaotic. Later that day, when they heard a disturbance on the dock and the sounds of gunshots, the Klinghoffers and other passengers paid little attention to the noise. They assumed it was another movie scene.

But when four armed hijackers came aboard shouting orders, everyone realized, in terror, that it was the real thing. The four terrorists were from the Palestine Liberation Front. They took the ship hostage and demanded the release of 50 Palestinian prisoners in Israeli jails.

They commanded the ship to set sail.

At one point the passengers (who numbered at least 400) were ordered to lie down flat on the dining room floor. One of the passengers, a Klinghoffer friend, did lie down on the floor, as ordered, face down. She had in her hands a pencil and a dinner menu. Employing her excellent artistic talent, she drew sketches of the faces of the terrorists, and of their weapons. There was no question that she put her life in danger by doing so.

It was not long after the ship was under way on the Mediterranean that, as reported, the frustrated Leon shouted at his captors. His shouting was later called a "provocation", and in front of his horror-stricken wife he was fatally shot and then, still in his wheelchair, thrown overboard into the sea.

Some of the friends in the Klinghoffer group, as well as other witnesses, commented on the encouragement that members of the crew gave to the terrorists, possibly a general "Italian pro-Palestinian political attitude" that was borne out later by official actions dealing with the apprehended terrorists.

The story of the hijacking was made into a TV movie called "Voyage of Terror." And a highly controversial opera based on the story called "The Death of Klinghoffer" was briefly presented and moved into obscurity until it was recently revived.

I called upon Marilyn, her daughters, and friends, and offered our temple sanctuary for Leon's funeral. It was accepted and it thus became my sad duty to eulogize Leon. I insisted there be no TV cameras in the temple and refused to permit even one that would serve the "pool" of media networks. I felt that this was a family funeral, not a media event. I did not object to small handheld audio-recorders. Apparently much of the recording was broadcast to the nation.

I spoke of Leon, of his wife and daughters, and I emphasized that his death, cruel and bestial, was a "Holocaust of One." Later on, I was both praised and criticized for the coining and usage of that phrase.

I referred to the "three miracles" in my eulogy. One was the fact that the terrorists had been apprehended by American fighter planes that succeeded in forcing down an Egyptian airliner in Sicily that was to have carried them to safety. The second miracle was the amazing fact that, like the Biblical Jonah, Leon Klinghoffer's body was washed up on the Syrian shore. The third miracle was that Syria, no friend of the Palestinians or the Jews, gave the body to the United States authorities. "The sea ... and the Syrians ... gave up their dead."

The body of Leon Klinghoffer was given a dignified hero's reception when it was returned to America. Our funeral cortege had an amazing, thunderous military procession and escort from the temple to the cemetery in New Jersey. As we proceeded, the city streets were lined with hundreds of caring people who waved small American flags as we passed.

In all of my years as a Rabbi in New York City, I believe I have officiated at burials in nearly every cemetery in the New York area. Yet this one, that contained the Klinghoffer family plot, was totally new to me. It was very small and very intimate, located on a commercial street in Kenilworth, New Jersey. I came upon it only one more time, four months later following the death and funeral service for Marilyn Klinghoffer who died at Lenox Hill Hospital after the cancer had spread irretrievably to other vital organs of her body. Although the daughters were distraught in their compounded grief and wanted to continue radical prolongation efforts, her mother, Rose Windwehr, could not bear her daughter's further suffering and begged them to "let Marilyn go."

Years later, when CBS News called concerning my opinion of the capture of Abu Abbas, the leader of this tragedy, I did not even know that coalition forces in post-war Iraq had apprehended him. When asked my thoughts on the matter, my harsh but honestly felt words were something to the effect: "The murderous bastard should be tried and convicted by the American judiciary."

Both of the daughters, the United States, and this Rabbi, refused to accept his protestation of innocence. He said he didn't do the actual shooting or "tossing." He said the killing was a mistake for which he was sorry.

None of us has accepted his apology.

It was small comfort, but when he died, he died in captivity.

God Is a Question Mark

A CONCEPT of God has always been a problem for me.
My extensive Jewish/Hebrew education was not religious. Attendance at Hebrew school, five times a week, Sunday through Thursday, had little or no connection with any temple or synagogue and attendance at services was truly never an issue. I rarely went to Shabbat services

I started Hebraic instruction when I was eight or nine years old. The school was an independent Hebrew school, which turned out to be terrible. There was no discipline and as a result, constant bad behavior. There were elderly, overbearing, old-fashioned teachers. Tuition was collected in cash every Sunday morning, except from my father, the holdout, who insisted on paying by check.

The atmosphere was horrendous. Discipline was offered in the form of yelling and slapping. My parents took me out and arranged home tutorial for me with a truly sweet, kindly old gentleman who had retired from the position of Hebrew school principal across the Mystic River in Chelsea. He was a wonderful pedagogue. I admit openly that I grew to love him and always felt that the love was returned. But that love gave me much pain. Though our sessions were scheduled from four to six p.m. every day (except Friday and Saturday) and on Sunday early afternoon, the clock, the time, the hours meant nothing to him. He adored teaching. At the window I could see my friends gathering, my sisters with their friends. But there was no way I had the nerve to tell him that 6:00 p.m. had come and gone. So I simply suffered it through but learned my Hebrew.

I studied with him till he died.

After his death, my dad enrolled me in a synagogue Hebrew school. Our teacher was a German Jew who had fled the Holocaust, somehow getting himself and his paralyzed wife out of danger and to the United States in time. He was also an instructor in mathematics at Harvard University. He understood our needs and discipline in his class was rarely a problem. Most of us were highly motivated to learn and we deeply appreciated his respect for us.

A good class and a fine teacher was a special match. This continued for three years. We all wanted it to go on but sixth grade was the next step and had nothing special about it.

But by then, for me, the die was cast. I loved my Hebrew studies. After bar mitzvah and sixth grade graduation, some of us went on to attend public high school (Boston Latin) and take a full-time curriculum at the Hebrew Teachers' College High School known as the Prozdor. "Prozdor" literally means "corridor", implying a corridor to the Hebrew Teacher's College (High School and College, lately renamed simply, Hebrew College) a place that defined itself as "a secular institution of higher Jewish learning." A substantial number of my peers attended both Harvard University and "HTC" at the same time. My Hebrew background enabled me to advance rapidly so that my public school and Hebrew school grade levels became equal and I graduated from Harvard University and the Hebrew Teachers' College in the same week.

Some of our teachers were ritually observant, but I believe they were in the minority. There were no religious services, no ceremonies, just lots of Hebraic learning. From the very beginning all classes were conducted in Hebrew. I had a jump-start on the Hebrew classes because the prior summer I had attended one of the Ramah camps where nearly everything was conducted in Hebrew.

In all my years of Hebrew school we had studied language, Hebrew as the language of the Bible, modern, medieval and ancient Hebrew literature, and the intricacies of Hebrew grammar. We absorbed mountains of Hebrew vocabulary. But rarely did we delve into God or theology, and seldom into Jewish philosophy. We studied Eretz Yisrael (to become Israel); we studied Zionism, its history and literature. We learned about the history of Chasidism, the multitude of messianic movements, the wanderings of our people over the globe, but never did we discuss the meaning of God or the different interpretations of Judaism current in Jewish life. We studied past and present, but never theology. If we studied medieval Jewish history and vicariously witnessed its philosophical effervescence, we were studying history, not the religion of our people.

The amazing thing was that we never felt or even discussed the lack of this discussion. We came from a variety of Jewish backgrounds but those differences were never part of our pedagogic experience.

Beneath it all, within it all, and above it all was a shared love for the Jewish people, the Jewish world experience, Jewish history, and that amazing hydra-headed, glowing creation of our people: Judaism. We literally rejoiced in its greatness of scope, of understanding, its tenacity, its resistance to structure and definition.

All this was deeply satisfying to me because I never believed in a "personal" God. I had studied too much Jewish history to be able to believe in a God who "cared," or one who "acted" in human history. Jewish history was filled with unspeakable pain. Its enormous triumphs were triumphs of the spirit and of the intellect, triumphs of the survival of community life.

In the tragedies that took place in my own life and in the life of my family, the conclusion was simply logically inescapable: there was, and is, no all-powerful God who watched over the universe, or humanity, or history.

But that does not mean that there is no God.

It means that for some of us who want to hold, however tenuously, a concept of God, that concept has to mean different things than an "all powerful doer" or "creator."

Having a fuzzy notion of God, anathema to one of my professors at seminary, is not out of line. For me God is a question mark. I don't know, and I don't have to know what God is. I can, on the basis of a great deal of Jewish thought and tradition, reject any anthropomorphic or anthropopathic conception of God.

I found that in order to give my problematic groping a "Jewish foundation" or "Jewish validity" I could find support in the writings of Philo, Maimonides, Spinoza (who should never have been banned), even a bit of the mysticism of Buber, Fackenheim and certainly Kaplan and Rubenstein, and even in some of the more mystical moments of anti-anthropomorphism of the Hebrew Bible from Pentatuch (Torah) to the books of the Wisdom Literature—especially Job and Ecclesiastes.

In order to be a Rabbi, bona fide and valid, I had to do battle with the "prayer book", a book in Hebrew and in English translation that constantly referred to God in anthropomorphic and anthropopathic terminology.

Once I left the supervision of a Rabbi who was my senior and mentor, and had my own solo pulpit at the Village Temple, this battle became public at every Shabbat service. I would substitute brief literary and philosophical readings for many prayer book passages. I would read and stop and reinterpret a prayer. I did everything I could to express and present a rationalist/mystic viewpoint of theology I carried through even at lifecycle ceremonies. I habitually carried a pile of page-marked books to the pulpit to be inserted and read during the service.

My manner of worship leadership might have been disturbing to some but, in truth, gave me enormous satisfaction. I found I was speaking not only out of the honesty of my own soul but was evoking responses in great numbers of people who had theological problems with the prayer book and much of religious institutional behavior as well.

I loved what I was doing and found an enormous favorable response to what I was doing. No reward for heartfelt effort and work could have been greater. And it was lovely to note that on a sheer pragmatic level, membership at the Village Temple increased by 300 percent and eventually membership at my subsequent uptown Temple by 600 percent.

I write these words with pride; they are not declarations of self-aggrandizement. For me, the battle goes on. I am constantly distressed by the fundamentalist approach to religion and religious behavior so rampant in the world today. It exists everywhere and has even spiritually invaded areas of the Reform Movement with its simple rigidities, its unproven certainties, and pseudo-spiritual declarations.

It is one of the world's understatements that religious fundamentalism has increased exponentially in the Muslim, Christian and Jewish worlds, adding a blind power to the fundamentalisms that already existed.

There is nothing wrong with spiritual uncertainty! It's disturbing to note that, having said that, there is a touch of courage and rebellion needed to proclaim it. In a world filled with uncertainty—cosmologically, politically and historically—it should be said with ease and trippingly on the tongue. Spirituality, and even the imaging poetry of ancient ritual, belongs to the seekers, doubters, and questioners as much as to the dogmatic and committed and unquestioning.

Honest spiritual uncertainty is for me and for many others a necessary challenge within the framework of the religious life of the Jewish people. I proffer that it is important to many non-Jews as well, but there is just so much with which one Rabbinic mind and heart can deal.

The Pothole Paradox

HE was a retired colleague. He called me early in the week. I could hear it in his voice: the terrible distress and anxiety; the humility with which he was asking a favor, the hope and despair in the same jumble of sentences and breath.

His daughter had just given birth to a beautiful baby boy. But the baby seemed to be doomed. Meconium aspiration: I had never heard the words before, but they mean that the baby in the womb passes feces that are absorbed into its lungs, a condition that after birth can asphyxiate the infant. Part of the treatment was to keep the baby totally sedated, near comatose. If the lungs could not be cleared, the next step would be drastic, invasive surgery on the little one's thorax.

For this, much blood was needed. I had once called for blood donations at a Shabbat service for an emergency and the response was heartwarming and wonderful. I told him not to worry about blood. I would announce the emergency call on Friday night and there would be plenty of donations.

I felt his sigh of relief and accepted his warm thanks. I made some calls to be sure that my response would not go unheeded. The answers were humane and caring.

On Thursday he called again. His voice was upbeat. "Don't make an emergency appeal from the pulpit," he said. "There's no need for blood because there was no need for surgery."

Research on the part of the staff at the hospital discovered that a unique vacuum-like machine could help. That machine was in another hospital way uptown. An ambulance arrived to transport the little boy to the other hospital. He was strapped into the small pediatric gurney and the trip began.

New York City, especially in winter, can claim more potholes in its streets than any city in the world. It has to do with the seepage of moisture beneath the asphalt and the tremendous pressures exerted by the repeated freezing and melting of the water. The ambulance driver was as careful as he could be as he was well aware of his precious cargo. But he could not avoid every single pothole. The ambulance bumped along, at times mercilessly; or was it mercifully? The constant jostling and rattling, the continuing bumping and grinding of the vehicle dislodged the meconium clogging the infant's lungs. He vomited it all up and out. The roughness of the ride on New York's Streets possibly proved more effective than the most precise, sensitive technical medical engineering that the human mind could devise. The baby was now breathing well and subsequent x-rays showed that his lungs were clear. He was saved.

After that amazing turn of events, I was one Manhattan Village dweller who would never again complain about the condition of New York City's roads.

The Man Who
Was Jesus

IT was not quite 5 o'clock in the morning when my telephone rang. A young man whom I knew was on the line.

"I heard your voice. You were speaking to me. I have a message for you. I must see you. I must speak to you. Where are you now?"

In my semi-sleepy state, I determined that his call was not a life-and-death emergency.

"Please wait," I said. "Call me back at eight."

He called me back promptly at eight a.m.

"I must see you, there is so much I have to tell you. I know that you were speaking to me. It was not a hallucination. It was your voice and everything you said was directed at me."

The caller was not hallucinating and had heard my voice. His only error was that I was talking to an audience on the airwaves and not exclusively to him.

A sister synagogue in Manhattan used to sponsor a Jewish radio program called "The Message of Israel." That program disappeared long ago. Taped sessions would be broadcast all over the country at many different hours. I believe that the principle of non-profit religious broadcasting was that free time was given to a program if the station had time available. Those available hours could be in the wee hours of a pre-dawn morning.

I had taped a number of talks through the years and I might have recalled once actually tuning in at the right time and station to catch myself on the air. Apparently old tapes were broadcast a number of times throughout the years. I never really knew when my voice and thoughts might be heard over the airwaves, save for this one time.

They seemed to be a promising young couple. She was striking, with dark eyes and dark hair, always impeccably dressed and precisely spoken. She had been a Lebanese Christian who had converted to Judaism and came to services often. Eventually she began to attend in the company of an equally striking young man. His looks were nearly a total contrast to hers. He was blonde and light, almost albino. His way of expressing himself was also measured and precise and expressed his interest in possible conversion as well. He supported himself by his work as a nightclub photographer.

So often we meet people who seem normal and restrained on the surface. So often that restraint and control masks a deep inner confusion and turmoil. One never knows what thought or incident will open the sluice gates to the outpouring of emotion or to the total loss of control.

I set a time for him to come to my study. He showed up precisely on time. His companion was with him. He was dressed, as I had often seen him, in a light suit and shirt. He looked exhausted and ragged.

Draped over his shoulders was a huge white linen bed sheet, like a flowing cape. In his hands was a ceramic jug. He said it was filled with holy water. He was sure now that he was Jesus and he had a message for the world. He wanted guidance from me as to how that message should be disseminated to humanity. He would follow whatever I said, because he had heard my voice in the middle of the dark night. His girlfriend, the dark-eyed woman, concurred that it was true; she too had heard my voice on the radio.

Only then did it occur to me that it was indeed my voice they really heard, on an isolated late-night re-broadcast of one of the audiotapes I had long ago recorded for the "Message of Israel."

I was not sure what to do, but felt that given my "hallucinatory" power over him, I could buy some time to figure it out.

My wife Meryl was worried that he could become violent. Who knows what anyone might do in the midst of a full-blown psychosis? I had pooh-poohed her fears. I knew them both. I told him to go home, get some rest, and return to me in two hours.

I called a psychiatrist with whom I served on the board of a social service organization. "Yes," he said, "he could turn violent. You must convince him to turn himself in voluntarily to Bellevue Psychiatric Hospital. You must play along with his fantasy. Don't negate what he says."

He and the woman returned in precisely two hours. By now, everyone in the Temple knew that something strange was underway.

"Rabbi, there's a man in a flowing cape carrying a bottle of holy water waiting to see you," said one of the office staff. "Shall I call the police?"

"Just send him up to me, but not to my study, to the chapel and have Greg [the building superintendent] there also."

The man came to the chapel. There was a certain pathetic majesty in his good looks, his cape, his holy water and the look of sublime stress and emotional exhaustion on his essentially handsome face. His woman friend was again by his side. Not a thread out of place. Perfectly groomed. She spoke first and indicated that there must be some truth to this vision of his.

A whole group of their friends had come by their apartment to see him. They listened to him speak and were most encouraging. They seemed to believe him and his message and they liked the holy water he had gently splashed upon them with his hand. They felt that, strange as it was, there was really something to all this.

Without meaning to be cruel or undermining, I "played along with the fantasy" but I gave that "playing along" a directive twist.

"The time has come for you to give your message to the world, but you really must do it right. I'm going to give you the taxi fare and you must go down to Bellevue Hospital and there you must spread your message. Convince the people there. Tell them what you have to say. That is the best place to begin. Once you have convinced them, the next step is easy. The next step is to speak to everyone."

He did it. He took a cab. He voluntarily entered Bellevue. I did not hear from him for a few days. He then called me at home.

"I don't like it here."

"No," I said. "You must be patient. It takes time. Don't give up on them so soon."

I don't know how they treated him. I don't know if they administered electro-convulsive therapy, or medical tranquilization, or psychotherapy or all three or combinations of each one.

I never saw him, or her, again. I tried to make contact. Phone calls and messages went unanswered. Her apartment had been vacated.

I do admit to looking over my shoulder occasionally walking home at night.

In Basketball It's Called "The Give and Go"

MY son was preparing, endlessly, to become a "specialized" surgeon. Four years of medical school were followed by five years of general surgical residency in NYC, which, in turn, were followed by two years of plastic surgery residency at Georgetown Medical Center, which preceded a one-year fellowship at Beth Israel—Deaconness Hospitals in Boston in hand surgery. That final year was under the tutelage of one of the world's finest and most famous hand surgeons.

One morning he was seeing patients at the shared Boston office. A giant entered the room. He had blond hair, a blond moustache and stood at six feet nine inches tall. My son recognized him at once as the great Larry Bird, star forward of the Boston Celtics, who had spurred his team on to several NBA championships and who was elected MVP for three seasons.

I admired Larry Bird. He was a magnificent, talented, clever, intelligent, charismatic player and team leader. My son knew of my vast admiration for him and thus an internal struggle took place within his soul. He knew it would be most unprofessional to ask for Bird's autograph, but he also knew how much pleasure it would give me. Professionalism won out; he treated the star's hand and watched him leave.

The next patient was a nun. She was of the older generation who still wore the traditional habit. As my son was examining her, he mentioned the regret he felt that he had not requested Larry Bird's autograph, even though it would have given his father great pleasure. At that moment the nun pulled a slip of paper out of her bag. While both were in the waiting room, she had asked Larry Bird for an autograph. He complied graciously, wrote a note and signed it.

With indescribable generosity and sweetness she handed the note to my son and said, "Please, please give this to your father." When my son demurred, she said that she would not be happy unless he took it and sent it along to his dad.

By the time my son visited me next, he had framed the note for posterity and with great satisfaction presented it to me. I accepted with enormous pleasure.

The autographed note gracing the shelves of this Rabbi's study reads:

"*To Sister Mary, Best Wishes, Larry Bird.*"

I wrote to Sister Mary. I don't know if she ever received my letter of warm thanks. I never heard from her.

I've always wanted her to know that her name and act of kindness occupy a place of honor in a rabbi's study.

I also wanted Larry Bird to know that with one gracious act he accomplished a double "mitzvah" for the servants of two faiths.

But She Looked Like My Mother

ICOULD not help but feel empathetic toward her. Physically, she reminded me of my mother.

She wanted a husband.

She had met the man of her dreams at a place in the Catskills, at a lovely, simple resort nestled in the hills.

She felt he had made promises to her. She believed those promises. He had wanted to marry her, but he left her. She believed she had a right to confront him but she couldn't do it alone. She was lonely, helpless and vulnerable. She needed assistance and accompaniment. Surely, as a Rabbi, I would have compassion and concern. Surely, I would help.

I told her I would truly think it over. Somehow she had both my Temple number and my home number and so she called to remind me. She called to noodge me. She called and called and called. When I came home late one evening, there she was in the lobby of my building waiting to talk to me, to ask me to help her speak to the man she wanted to marry who had promised to marry her.

I gave in. My naïve sense of compassion assured me that such dogged persistence must be founded on some inner motivational truth. She told me the address of his place of business and we met there the following morning. We climbed the stairs to the loft where he processed textiles. We entered through the large rolling iron gates. We found him. I introduced myself.

As we stood before him, I saw a rather pleasant fellow turn into an enraged maniac the moment he looked at her.

"You are here again!"

Then he turned to me. "Rabbi, yes, I know her. We were once at a place in the Catskills. I was polite to her. I offered her a ride home. I never promised her anything. I was simply being a kind gentleman. Her imagination carried her away. You are the fourth rabbi she has brought around. Something is wrong, terribly wrong. I never want to see her again. Take her away. Please take her away!" And then to the woman: "Never come here or call me again. Leave me alone! Next time I'll call the police!"

She looked at me and rolled her eyes as if he were the crazy one.

I couldn't believe I had gotten into this. But she looked like my mother. That's what did it.

Back down on the street she went one way. I went another.

I never saw or heard from her again.

The Phantom
of Masada

DURING the course of my career, a great joy and inspirational
pleasure has been my twenty temple group tours to Israel. Each
one was filled with its own set of adventures and involvements. We've
gone through times of peace, uncertainty and Intifada. We've added on
trips to England, Egypt, Jordan, Holland and France.

Each time our goal was to explore the land fully, from its northernmost
tip at the border with Lebanon to its southernmost point, Eilat on the
Red Sea. We even traveled the Sinai Desert to Santa Katerina and
Yamit on the Mediterranean shore, when it was still in Israeli hands.

We visited border outposts and great cities, ancient archeological
sites as well as locations important to modern history. We stood at
places where the stories made the tears flow and at sites where the heart
almost burst with pride.

We truly toured the land: the kibbutzim, the Druze villages, Arab
areas, Orthodox Jewish places, Reform Jewish enclaves, citadels of
learning, hospitals, private homes, military bases, ancient and modern
fields of battle, artists' colonies, luxury hotels, the Galil, the Negev, the
Sharon plain, the deserts, the mountains, the Red, Dead, and Med
Seas as well as the Sea of Galilee.

For so many of us, the State of Israel is an inspiring dream-come-true.
What the state and her people have accomplished in spite of mighty wars
and murderous terrorism is remarkable. And the absorption of millions
of immigrants in the establishment of universities, industries, intensive
agriculture, cultural attainments, centers of scholarship, research, and

amazing scientific advance—all of it overwhelms the mind. I cannot help but declare that I am an ardent Zionist, a lover of Israel. My heart breaks that in recent years it has become at times so very difficult to bring American travelers to witness its inspiration and wonder.

Through the years we had over 70 ceremonies of Bar and Bat Mitzvah in various settings, from the ancient ruins of Korazin, the Wall in Jerusalem, the hills of the Judean Desert to the shore of the Dead Sea and high atop the mountain of Masada.

Psychologists speak of "peak" moments in human life. Some took place during our many trips to Israel. My assumption is that a "peak moment" is one that is never forgotten, whose thrill returns to the soul again and again.

Such a peak moment was on our second trip when four of our Temple children were undergoing the ceremony of Bar and Bat Mitzvah on Masada, Herod's ancient mountain fortress looking down over the Dead Sea. There, the Jewish zealots held out against the vast Roman forces for three years. Before suffering a crushing defeat, they fulfilled a suicide pact.

The weather, even for the desert, was magnificent, sunny, bright, and breezy. Our service was held in the ruins of the ancient Masada Zealot Synagogue. As the children helped conduct the service, chant the blessings and read from the Torah, one of those awesome Israeli Phantom jet fighter planes began to fly around the mountain on the same level as we were. The noise was overwhelming, deafening. But we resolutely continued the service. The stiff breeze blew the ends of our tallitot up high, but that was no bother compared to the din of the fighter jet. Its fuselage gleamed in the sun, the blue Star of David clearly visible and gorgeous. The pilot kept circling us. We kept praying.

Finally, I looked up. His path of flight was so close to the mountain, I could see his face.

As I looked up, he looked up at me and at our group. Then he tipped his wing. There is no doubt in my mind that he was saying, like any good Jewish passerby, *Mazel Tov!* He knew what we were doing and he was following a most gracious, thrilling, Jewish etiquette, wishing us well. My eyes locked into his eyes in the distance. He dipped. I waved. He dipped his wing once more and flew off into the distance. The mighty roar had become a silent joy and the thrill of his visit permeated each remaining moment of our four ceremonies.

Before we had left the United States, I had personally prepared the children for their ceremonies. I was not pleased with the regularly assigned Haftarah (prophetic reading) because I wanted something more appropriate to the time and place. So I chose the 37th Chapter of the prophet Ezekiel, the wonderful message delivered when the prophet imagines himself in the valley of dry bones. The voice says to him, "Can these bones live?" And the prophet responds, "O Eternal One thou knowest."

The bones come together, they are given flesh and sinew and life and breath and they arise as a mighty host and return to the Land of Israel.

The prophet may not have known it, but a stupendous metaphor had been created for modern post-Holocaust Jewish history and the heroic founding of the State of Israel.

The children read and chanted the lines, the flight of the jet having injected life and meaning into the words of the prophet.

When the service ended, we turned and found a small gate with an inscription: "On this spot were found ancient fragments from the ruins of the synagogue, fragments from the 37th Chapter of the Book of Ezekiel."

Even now, years and years later, I get a chill down my spine.

The Rabbi Who Became A Ghost

AFTER dozens of years of rabbinic service, the time had come for a break. Meryl and I chose to spend our sabbatical on a cruise around the world. I had no desire to serve as ship's rabbi but simply to be another pampered, coddled passenger.

We booked a cruise of 97 days, one that left the U.S. in January and returned in April. The itinerary included over 30 ports-of-call on all continents. In spite of the miserable poverty that we witnessed in many parts of the world the trip was soul-filling. We particularly loved the plains of Africa, where we saw every kind of wild animal roaming freely on the Masai Mara Reservation.

Off the coast of Brazil a fax came from my office. My loyal and hard-working administrative assistant had protected me from numerous communications but this one had to come through. Immediately, upon receipt of the fax, I was to call a special number at the White House in Washington, D.C., and though my assistant tried to convince the caller from the West Wing that I was completely unavailable, the voice said imperiously: "Lady, this is the White House calling!" She had to give in.

At personal, astronomical expense, I called the number. It was indeed the White House. I gave them my ship's number and stateroom extension and they called me back.

I had been contacted by a member of the speech-writing staff of the Vice President of the United States. Within the coming week, the Vice President was scheduled to give a speech in Jerusalem on the occasion of the 50th Anniversary of the State of Israel. A speech was needed. Could I please write one immediately and fax it to them?

I was astonished, overwhelmed, honored, and galvanized to go to work. I started writing that instant and did not stop until it was done. I love the State of Israel and am in perpetual awe of its meaning for both Jewish and human history. I tried to include my deepest emotions, feelings that I hoped the second-highest official of the United States of America would express.

I needed a typist. The cruise director of the ship was a busy young woman but she volunteered to type my manuscript. After the second editing, it was ready to be faxed and was sent and received. I hoped it would be useful.

Weeks after my return to New York, I received a letter of thanks from the White House staff. The envelope included a full copy of the Vice President's presentation. With the exception of the opening salutations (Mr. Prime Minister, President, Mayor, etc.) and a few minor changes, my words, my thoughts, and my heart's outpouring were expressed.

I was deeply proud, but political correctness demanded that my pride be maintained in silence.

Enough time has passed that the "ghost" can take on living flesh.

The Prince and the Poet

SAM Soloff, a former president of the Temple, took his wife and three daughters on a trip to Europe.

They were all having an enjoyable journey, except for the youngest daughter. She enjoyed nothing and complained about everything. She was a beautiful teenager with an attitude. Her list of grievances grew and continued until they came to the small kingdom of Monaco where they visited and toured the palace.

She loved the palace. This was what she wanted to see. This was where she wanted to be. This was where she would like to spend her life.

Her mother took note.

Some time after their return to America, mother took pen in hand and, without her youngest daughter knowing, wrote a letter in her daughter's name to the Prince of Monaco at his address in the palace. The prince was a young single gentleman.

Time went by. No answer came.

Mother took pen in hand once again. She poured her heart into a second letter in her daughter's name, and sent it off to the palace.

A few weeks later a call came to the Soloff home. "This is Monsieur Jacques, secretary to the Prince of Monaco. May I speak to Deborah?"

She got on the phone. "The secretary to the Prince of Monaco? Yeah, sure you are."

"The Prince will be in New York City in two weeks and would like you to join him at a party he is giving at his [very elegant] hotel. His limousine will pick you up at your apartment house lobby at six p.m."

Mother then revealed all to her youngest child. A sense of combined doubt and amazement filled the air at home for the next two weeks.

The day before the appointed time the secretary to the Prince called again to remind them of the pick-up by limo and the party rendezvous.

Daughter was ready. The limo came exactly on time and took her to the elegant hotel and to the equally elegant party of the Prince.

When he met her face-to-face he was gracious and warm to her.

She asked him, "You must receive buckets of mail every day, why did you pick out mine? I'm just a simple, nice, Jewish girl."

"I was deeply impressed," said he "by the poetry you wrote."

Another triumph for Mother!

When eleven p.m. came around, the party crowd began to dwindle. The Prince told her he would take her home in his limousine. He took her to her building. He escorted her inside her lobby. He embraced her and kissed her goodnight.

She never saw or heard from him again.

Gaffes I Have Made

I

IT took only one embarrassing mistake to teach me the necessity of never getting a name wrong in a ceremony of any sort.

Fortunately, it was early on in a budding career. I was a student Rabbi in my final year at the rabbinic seminary. I was required to have "solo" rabbinic experience. Before school began, I was called for an "unveiling", the dedication of a tombstone at the grave of a loved one that takes place within the first year following burial. Somehow the name of the deceased never reached the inner core of my thought process. I do believe that I mentioned the name of a living loved one, instead of the entombed soul. A never-ending source of surprise to me was that the family was either too overwhelmed or too kind-hearted to mention my mistake to me. I learned of it months later from other members of the Temple.

II

IT HAD been a day of abominably slow traffic, dealing with heartache and a host of other distracting frustrations.

When I finally got to the hospital to co-officiate with a mohel at a ceremony of circumcision, I saw the friendly, familiar faces of the family. I uttered the first silly words that rose to my lips: "What did you have?"

III

I HAD a wedding scheduled for late spring. The groom called me in
early January with overtones of panic in his voice:

"Rabbi, we must have the wedding as soon as we can. This week, if
possible." It was possible.

We met in the chapel. Only the bride, the groom, two friends as
witnesses, and two sets of parents were present.

The bride's mother was very upset. She wept audibly during the
whole ceremony.

I wanted to comfort her. A miasma of blockheadedness must have
settled on my mentality. I cringe when I relive the words of "comfort"
that I offered her.

"Don't be sad; you're not losing a daughter. Before you know it, there
will be grandchildren!"

All talk stopped. A dead silence permeated the chapel. Wordlessly,
everyone went for their coats to move on to the wedding dinner.

IV

I CANNOT forget the beautiful, outdoor Labor Day wedding at
which I officiated in the foothills of the Berkshires in New England.
The setting of the wedding was magnificent: a sloping green lawn
of a beautiful home in the hills, a soft breeze, classical quartet, and
large loving family added touching and beautiful ambience to the
proceedings.

Fourteen years later, I shared the ceremony of the Bar Mitzvah
of their first-born son. During the proceedings, I could not help but
comment on the beauty of the Bar Mitzvah boy's parents' wedding
ceremony.

I had either simply forgotten or had totally repressed the fact that
they were in the midst of rather unpleasant divorce proceedings.

The Conversion

L ESLIE. There was no way to describe her. She was stunning. In her early thirties, she was a large-boned woman but everything about her was in proper proportion. Her hair was dark, silky, shorter than a pageboy, beautifully neat and groomed with not a strand out of place; she wore low pumps and close fitting, elegant clothes; her skin, above all, was pearly and perfect. And she wanted to convert to Judaism.

There was no boyfriend, no fiancé, no husband, as is so often the case. For a number of years she wanted to convert because she felt at home in the synagogue. She had attended a large uptown congregation and just bought an apartment in the Village near the Temple. She wanted to establish and nurture her roots in her new home, new neighborhood, and new community.

She was extraordinarily well educated, an honors graduate of one of the famous elite "Seven Sisters" women's colleges. She held an important position with one of the large national banks that had its headquarters in downtown Manhattan. Adopting the Jewish faith made her feel another piece of her existence would be put in the right place at the right time.

She was an excellent student. She attended the lectures, read the texts, faithfully came to Shabbat services, and kept her weekly appointment with me without interruption or excuse.

As our academic relationship moved into its sixth month, I came to know her well. In addition to all her obvious good and solid qualities, she was pleasant, chatty and affable.

A very successful fortyish widower in the congregation noticed her at services. He asked me about her. I gave him only very general information: yes, she seemed to be single. Would I ask her if he might call her to go out to dinner? Yes, I would. I did. She would. They did, but only once.

My acquaintance with Leslie occurred long before the Gay Rights Movement began. Urban legend claims it began when the New York City Police raided one of the gay bars in the Village and the men fought back. Their civil rights as free and independent non-criminal human beings had been invaded. Lawsuits and counter lawsuits were filed. The media zoomed in. A most important revolution with enormous and far-reaching impact was born.

The implications of that revolution reached everywhere, as the world knows, even the hallowed halls of every area of the religious communities of the earth. It was not long before its implications reached into my own life as well.

My own sexual orientation is undeniably "straight." Yet that did not forestall a number of occasions on which I had been "approached": some subtle, some blatant, from summer camp as a counselor to my years at Hebrew University. I had little understanding of the issues and little tolerance, and I acted accordingly. I tried not to hire or employ those whose gender orientation was "suspect." It was amazing to me how many fit that category. I will probably be excoriated for expressing this, but it was astonishing to note how many gay people of every faith entered the clergy.

All of this astonished me until the time I was asked to serve on the "Ad Hoc Committee on Homosexuality in the Rabbinate" by the Executive Vice President of the Central Conference of American Rabbis. The only qualification for service was that I had to profess an open mind on the issue.

From the time I was asked until the time the national committee convened, I determined to do my homework and do it well. But the first step turned out to be a book written by a woman in the Temple who had had four sons, one of whom was gay. She had written about her experience with him and I found her story profound, loving, and moving. As a member of our Sisterhood she was invited to speak about her book but two days before the scheduled program, she died.

I was asked to review the book in her place. The start of the session, attended by her loved ones, was tearful. We had a few moments of memorial, and then I launched into my very favorable review of her book. I could not help but notice in the audience the presence of a number of older couples whose children, men and women, had never married. The total transformation of my thinking had begun.

After reading numerous texts, proliferating legal challenges, interviews with psychologists and psychiatrists in the congregation and beyond, I could not help but come to the conclusion that homosexuality was a natural, or "God-given" unavoidable biogenic and/or psychogenic condition. Some people had brown eyes. Some people had blue eyes. Some people were gay, while most people were straight. The question was not one of deviancy or abnormality or criminality, it was a matter of civil rights. Even without "biogenetic" assumptions, we live in a country of freedom and democracy. Even plain old choice is valid.

I brought my hard-won conclusions to the committee meetings. We met fourteen times over a four-year period. I found most of the meetings to be at least "three-aspirin" sessions, as I hadn't anticipated becoming the "flaming liberal" on the committee. Also, I was deeply moved by some of the anonymous pain-filled testimonials of gay colleagues who had lived their lives in fearful secrecy, anonymous testimonies obtained by gay members of our committee.

The success of the gay rights revolution was all around us: New York City housing policies, the sharing of corporate benefits, changes in federal and state legislatures, even the military (albeit with extreme reluctance and prejudice). Gay themes on national television, open gay involvement in the American political process, openly gay members of the legislature and then, the imprimatur of acceptance: inclusion of pictures and announcements of gay consecration ceremonies in the "Styles" wedding section of the New York Times.

How did all of this fare in confrontation with the Books of Leviticus and Deuteronomy in the Torah, which branded male homosexuality a "to-eva," an abomination? (Female homosexuality was considered with much greater "flexibility.") Some colleagues twisted and turned to deny the literal interdiction of the ancient texts. For me, I had to conclude that in all truth and honesty, the ancient texts were wrong. Those elements of society that branded AIDS as a "WOG" ("Wrath of God") punishment were as nonsensical to me as a consideration of cancer, or any other illness, as some kind of divine retribution or punishment. The human authors of the Bible did not have the medical information we do now.

The plenum of the CCAR overwhelmingly accepted our report and its liberal conclusions about accepting homosexuality! Out of what may have been hundreds of positive votes, I can recall only *one* that was vocally and publicly negative.

The world, for the most part, has moved on. Even a gay Episcopalian priest was raised to the level of Bishop, albeit amid much schismatic controversy in the world-church. And the Supreme Court, with its politically conservative makeup, voted to protect individual privacy in the matter of sexual activity.

But all of that came long after Leslie's conversion. If I "fix" people up, I never inquire how "things went", but the widower volunteered a rather quizzical comment. "That Leslie—she has some strange ideas about men!"

Leslie called soon after the "date." I was not prepared psychologically or emotionally for her question of so many years ago. How different my response would have been years later.

"Rabbi, would you officiate at a marriage of two women?"

In consternation, I answered that there was no such thing, either legally (still almost totally true) or religiously (not true at all for many of us now!).

I wish I had known or felt then what I know and feel now. I wish that I had been prepared to do then what I could do with relative ease now. I wish I had had a more open mind and a broader understanding that eventually I feel I achieved much later on.

I could feel the disappointment and even the despair at the other end of the telephone line. The conversation ended abruptly. I never saw Leslie again.

The Runaways

THEY were two young girls: pre-pubescent, very young-looking teenagers, talkative, engaging, quite frightened and out of money. They had been through their ceremonies of Bat Mitzvah and Confirmation together in their hometown of Pittsburgh. They were both high-strung, wound-up and obviously "high maintenance." After intense disagreements with their parents over a whole host of matters, they ran away from home. Their destination: Greenwich Village.

They had heard about the Village for years. Older siblings and cousins had been to off-Broadway shows there; they had enjoyed the folk singing clubs; the improv theatre groups; the crowds on the sidewalks; the ambience of the small random streets.

If they were going to run away, there was no destination more exciting or enticing.

They came by train and then subway and arrived in the dark of the early, cold, wintry morning hours. It was too cold to walk in the streets. Washington Square Park felt like the North Pole. They were not dressed warmly enough for the frigid weather. The halls of the New York University's downtown campus were closed everywhere. They checked into the nearest fleabag hotel they could find. The hotel was warm, but strange sounds emanated from every direction, moans, footsteps, hammering, off-key singing, and even a few gentle (and some not so gentle) knocks on the door. Fatigue ruled, but sleep was impossible. A tangible fear trembled in their souls with every knock, disturbance and sound. They had overpaid an enormous amount of demanded up-front cash for the dusty, infested room, and now little was left beyond what was needed for an inadequate, skimpy breakfast for two growing teenage girls.

When the sun rose, they finally slept for an hour or two. The bustling sounds of the streets and the comings and goings of hundreds of NYU students were comforting.

They awoke and hastily left their less than luxurious surroundings. Somehow, without much money in their pockets, inadequate clothing against the cold, and the non-caring attitude of the denizens of the streets, Greenwich Village had lost its romantic appeal. They wanted to go home.

What to do? They didn't have to walk very far. On 12th Street, one of them looked eastward: "Look! There's a Jewish star! It must be a synagogue! Let's go that way!"

They came, bedraggled, tired, and frightened, their eagerness for adventure and retribution against restrictive parents knocked out of them. They came and they wanted succor and relief and help to go home.

I was in my office. I had scheduled a great deal of what I felt was important work for that day. A good amount of it could not be postponed.

It was only moments before two hysterical young women were crying and pleading in my study. They gave me their home phone numbers. I called immediately. One set of parents was home. They were enormously relieved by my call. I gave them the Temple number and my home phone. The other couple was not at home and there was no message machine. I called numerous times. I called throughout the morning and early afternoon. I called the first couple and asked them to reach the other parents as soon as they could and give them the message that the girls were safe and that I was making arrangements to get them home. I could not leave my office, but arranged for lunch to be brought in for them. The girls were warm, well fed, and the hysteria dissolved into comfortable quiescence. All through the hours, both the secretary and I kept trying the other parents' telephone number in Pittsburgh.

There was no flight till early evening. My wife agreed to let the girls come home with me. When we came, she had prepared a lovely dinner for us. The plane reservations had been made and I had called for the car to be ready to drive the runaways to the terminal at Kennedy Airport.

The day had been emotionally stressful. Not only because of the plight of the runaway girls, but also because of some deep emotional entanglements and difficulties among members of the congregation. I could not postpone my attentiveness to those problems. Their situation only added further complications to a very difficult day.

When we reached my wife's delicious, teenage-oriented dessert, the phone rang. It must have been a ring like any other ring, but to my memory it was intensely loud and ominous.

The call was from the second set of parents whom I had tried to reach all day.

I had expected to be thanked for my care and concern. Not so. I was subjected to a vicious verbal diatribe. I was supremely bawled out. I was inconsiderate, unkind, irresponsible, unfeeling. How could I call one family and not call the other? How could I be so cruel and callous?

There were very few occasions in my 44-year rabbinic career in which I "lost it." This was one of them. I totally, completely, unavoidably, inevitably lost my cool. Instead of being understanding, forgiving, appreciative of their tension, I raised my voice and responded harshly, loudly, mercilessly. I reached a certain horrid crescendo when I declared that it was easy to see why their daughter had run away from such cruel, obtuse and destructive stupidity. They were intensely angry that the other couple had not reached them, and they had to call first and get the information and numbers from them. But "that New York City Rabbi" became the primary focus and cause of their anger.

As I look back, I don't think I could have tempered my outrage. A soft response would have been contemptuous and icy. As it was, I don't think it changed them, but it truly helped me.

The drive to Kennedy was silent. The runaway daughter of the parents who had excoriated me seemed to be hurt for them. I wish she could have been hurt for them before she decided to run away.

We came to the terminal. They boarded the plane. I had paid for the tickets out of my own pocket.

I did receive a check days later that reimbursed my costs.

In the envelope that held the checks then was a written diatribe against me and all Rabbis.

Not a word of thanks.

It was the only time that I ever received a check and neglected to send a thank-you note.

A Memorable Interfaith Lunch

IT is well known in the Village that the King of England gave important parcels of land to some churches before the American Republic was created. These churches, as well as other similarly blessed organizations, were incredibly wealthy. If one installed a magnificent new organ, another did so as well, seemingly not to be outdone.

A member of the Temple had grown extremely wealthy when he devised the legal procedures through which developers could lease church lands and thereupon build huge residential towers. These towers both impinged upon and altered the quaint landscape of the Village and were all immediate commercial successes.

That success further increased the wealth of the churches. The original congregations had mostly moved away. The new church buildings and renovations were inordinately lovely, but the pews seemed empty, void of the community that had originally enjoyed them.

Their ministers were particularly friendly and kind. They warmly welcomed synagogues to their neighborhood. Interfaith relations were consistently excellent.

One of the churches invited all the Village clergy, ministers, rabbis, priests, nuns and all their spouses and significant others to a lovely luncheon at which even Kosher food had been copiously provided.

The gathering was informal, high-toned, and elegant. My wife and I were seated at a table with two nuns who were charming, warm and friendly.

When dessert came, one of the nuns turned quietly to the other.

They exchanged comments that we could not hear, nodded to each other, and then turned to Meryl and me.

"Would you help us out? We need some explanations, if you don't mind."

We agreed immediately, though puzzled as to what this concerned.

"In our school lately, we have seen a proliferation of gestures. We dare not ask the priests what they mean. Can you, would you, tell us what they signify?"

Fortunately, conversation in the room was lively and the participants in the luncheon were focused on their own tables as the nuns proceeded each one in turn to:

A. Give us the finger—first with the index finger

B. Then with the middle finger

C. Then put their left fists inside the elbow area of the right arm

And

D. Do the same with the left fist in the crook of the right arm, with the middle finger raised straight up.

"What," they asked, "is the meaning of these gestures?" Did the use of the index finger imply a different connotation than the middle finger? Was it the same if the right fist was in the crook of the left arm? Was the extended finger in this case an intensified implication of the bent arm?

With Talmudic precision but sans demonstration, Meryl and I proceeded to explain each gesture one by one. The faces of the nuns deepened red, then turned purple. There was even a touch of green toward the end. With correctness and care, we told them what they thought they wanted to know. With an awkward reticence, they thanked us.

Dessert arrived. Our table was very quiet.

I did not see the nuns at the next interfaith luncheon, or, for that matter, at any interfaith event after that.

The Temple Bizarre

I HARDLY knew him. He was a singer who knew some Hebrew and was also one of the many unordained, uncertified, unofficial "cantors" who abound in New York City.

By coincidence we had officiated together at a celebrity wedding. The media had shown their accustomed zeal for widespread coverage of the event, in spite of strong pleas and attempts to preserve the privacy and dignity of the occasion. Adding to the notoriety, my co-officiating "cantor" was the son of a world-renowned singer.

Some time ago a cherished colleague had told me of some bizarre incidents in his career when he served as an Associate Rabbi at a big congregation in a large Midwestern city. He said that among the affluent young couples in the Temple there were "key club" parties and "swinger societies" galore. There were people whose life was seemingly aimless and uncreative and they had too much time and money available. He told us of one cool day when a woman in the Temple came to see him, warmly dressed in a full, rich, luxurious fur coat. She entered his office. With polite cordiality he asked her what was on her mind? She stood up, opened her coat, revealed a totally nude body beneath and said, "Rabbi, I want you!"

My colleague then told us breathlessly that he didn't remember what he said or did—his mind had suppressed it all—but somehow, desperately, he put her back into her coat, turned her around and got her out of his study.

All of this came to mind when that "cantor" called to set up an appointment to see me as soon as possible, within the hour if it could be done. Just beyond the hour he walked into my study. He was not naked under his coat, but his purpose was clear. He believed that I had shown him incredible warmth during the wedding ceremony. It may not have been as desperately expressed as the lady in the Midwest, but he "wanted me." My protestations of "straightness" seemed to be of no avail. Why wouldn't I deepen our relationship? It can happen only a few times in a lifetime. I should reveal my true self. Let life take its course. Be open! Be free! Don't let a thing of such beauty slip out of our hands!

Much like my colleague, my mind has suppressed the words and details that followed but somehow, in some way, I got him out of my study.

And out of my life.

Who Comforts the Rabbi?

A CLERGY person is literally constantly torn asunder by the tragedy in human existence.

Long ago I found the need to develop for myself a consistent theology that sought to make sense of our difficult world. One that I could meaningfully share with others; one that did not outrage my reason; one that I could offer when asked by those in the throes of anguish, pain and loss. One that was not puerile and meaningless.

The world, the universe, the universe of universes—all are haphazard occurrences. How much more so the vulnerability of human life.

In all of this chance, God is a question mark. That does not mean that God is absent. We just don't know what God is. I believe that it was Gertrude Stein once wrote: "There never was an answer, there is no answer, and there never will be an answer. And that's the answer."

I cannot claim to be an expert on the writings and teachings of Moses Maimonides (the Rambam) but I can claim that without the philosophic rationalist theological approach laid down by Maimonides in the Middle Ages, in his monumental attempts to reconcile the "Torah of Moses" with the "teachings of Aristotle." I could not be a traditionally religious Jew. His rationalism, his anti-anthropomorphism and anti-anthropopathism—his "via negativa" (assertions that we can speak only of what God is NOT)—enabled me to grasp a concept of God, creation, humanity and the universe that has been both simultaneously reasonable and mystical. This approach is anathema to most fundamentalist religion—whether Jewish, Christian or Muslim.

It has always been comforting for me to note that as there have been moderate rationalist theological directions in Judaism, so also have there been in various areas, at various times, in Christianity and Islam. For me, to speak of the "will of God" is to speak anthropomorphically about God. For me, even to speak of God's forgiveness is to speak anthropopathically about God. Both are rationally unacceptable to me.

For me, the formula is simple (but profound and complicated at the same time): God = Life +X. We cannot know even the totality of life. X, the unknown beyond life, is the direction into which we can put our prayer, our liturgy, our poetry.

The tragedies I have witnessed were not "God's will." I bristle at this assertion. It raises far more questions than it answers.

Good things happen, or are achieved. Bad things happen, or are the result of human malevolence.

The Holocaust rises above our ratiocinations. It was evil in so deep and wide a level, involving so many murderers and murderous methodic technology, that it defies description, explanation and categorization.

Elie Wiesel was 14 years old when he was brought to Auschwitz. His story, as told in "Night", seared my soul and transformed my life: "Never shall I forget that night, the first night in camp, which has turned my life into one long night, seven times cursed and seven times sealed." I would never forget the descriptions of his life and experiences in that concentration camp. And yet, Elie Wiesel went on to author over 30 books, to represent the creative best of the Jewish people, to receive the Nobel Prize for Peace and Job-like, to continue to inspire, lead, teach and epitomize the undying Jew of the 20th and 21ˢᵗ Centuries.

But reasoning on from the disaster of the Holocaust to personal or family tragedy, I find Richard Rubenstein's major work, "After Auschwitz: Essays in Contemporary Jewish Theology", extremely useful. He is one of the few theologians who, especially in this particular text, plays no games with words or thoughts. He faces the evil of the human sphere, the sense of angst and tragedy we have all known, and speaks in terms that are brutal and eloquent.

His overriding theological conclusion is that God is the "Holy Nothingness" out of which we came and to which, in death, we return. "Death," he writes, is "the Messiah", that which releases us from the pain of life and living.

I cannot help but react personally to his honesty. His outlook is bleak and I agree with his hard-won truths, but need a bit more joy than he gives emotionally or philosophically. While agreeing with his approach, I need to change only one word to offer the same truth, but with a sense of human hopefulness. Just a change of word helps: "God is the Holy *Everythingness*." This notion may echo the "Substance" of Spinoza or the naturalism of Kaplanian Reconstructionism but, I believe, philosophically changes nothing of Rubenstein, only the attitude within. It is a far happier statement for me, not so totally reductionist, nor so terribly and terrifyingly sad.

The power that created the universe, that created life, is a mystery. I feel that there is vision and poetry in that mystery. But there is also terror and angst.

This was my answer to a brilliant pediatrician whose baby had died inside her and, at least for the moment, when I spoke of my feeling, it seemed to calm and comfort her. I can't escape the notion that "theology" is the verbalization of our feelings.

Jewish theology and any theology, for that matter, must deal with the hideous reality of the Holocaust, the unleashed, purposeful, murderousness that engulfed an entire continent of nations, a murderousness that has been repeated a number of times on a lesser scale.

Into this framework of thought I have placed my attempts to comfort the families struck by unspeakable tragedies.

The many suicides I have eulogized and buried, particularly those of the inherently New York City genre, who have jumped from tall buildings all over the City and outer boroughs, but particularly those high structures that have altered the low-rise quaintness of Greenwich Village for years. They included a psychotherapist, a "closeted" gay man, one young highly accomplished nephew who visited his beloved aunt and uncle and jumped from their study window while they thought he was taking a nap (till they saw the police cars stream together in front of their building's entrance), the nonagenarian who didn't want to live if she couldn't do the things she loved, the young woman struck into deep depression by the results of an impending Internal Revenue Service audit.

The double deaths, of a loving grandparent couple who perished when driving after making a "bad turn" with the grandchildren in the backseat (seriously injured, but eventually fully healed), the fraternal twin brothers, their parents' only children, both gay and both dead of AIDS, the brothers—the older one who, first in his graduation class from an elite college, studied the tides of the bay so his body wouldn't be found and then jumped off one of the country's great bridges—the younger dead of AIDS a few years later.

The necessity, when possible, for families to identify the physical remains and the times when I was asked to do it for them.

The murder of nearly an entire family by a member of the family who had never before even handled a gun, who bought a rifle with ease, and who murdered her two children and herself.

The teenager who died of AIDS before the title of the illness was even invented; the young men whom I eulogized and buried long after the world became overly acquainted with AIDS.

Exactly one week after she was confined to a wheelchair because of MS, the death of a Broadway dancer who left young children behind.

The babies who have died because of physical difficulties.

The horrible deterioration of ALS, MS and CF again and again and again and again.

The teenagers who have drowned or been asphyxiated and perished from asthma, leukemia, Hodgkin's Lymphoma, and other forms of long-suffering cancers.

The young mother who died in childbirth, even though surrounded by every medical facility and procedure known to modern medicine, whose baby, given up for dead, began to breathe on its own and survived.

The beautiful 14 year old girl, talented and brilliant, born to her parents after eleven years of trying, who went to sleep with what seemed to be a simple headache and was found in the morning sleeping eternally.

The baby who died from a fall from a high, unprotected window and the sad, sad dissolution of the marriage since neither partner could continue to live together in their despair.

The plague of cancers of all kinds upon persons of all ages.

The young parents who have left young children behind; the youngsters whose lives and well-being were invaded by myeloma, and unknown undiagnosable causes.

The young mothers-to-be who lost their living babies in the last days of the nine-month pregnancy and who needed desperately the Jewish rituals of grief and healing.

The couples whose fetus' prenatal chromosome tests clearly indicated the need for pregnancy termination and who also needed grief counseling and ritual comfort.

The amazingly talented young sportsman, expert in athletics of all kinds, who was hit and killed by a bus while riding his bike.

The young fiancé killed accidentally by an out of control auto as he jogged in Central Park.

The sweet son and stepson who was traveling cross-country in his beloved old car, who stopped to nap in the cold high mountains of Utah and kept the heater on while he slept and died of carbon monoxide poisoning.

The beautiful portrait of the elderly grandmother's two young grandsons, smiling out of an illumined past, dead of AIDS and suicide.

One's heart breaks with sorrow. One's inner soul is shredded.

"What sustains you?" asked a grieving father. What sustains any priest, minister or rabbi overwhelmed with recurrent tragedies? I'm not sure that I can answer for others, or even for myself. But a mundane part of the answer seems to me to be that it is our job, our profession, our responsibility to try to give comfort. If that effort is crowned by some effectiveness, the resultant strength can be sustaining.

What sustains me? Does the scar tissue of an often broken heart give one strength?

Who comforts the rabbi?

As I found again and again: my wife and children. Their sympathy, their empathy, their love, their caring, their embraces.

I was fortunate to have that about me. That sustained me.

It must be said that some of the *Tales of the Village Rabbi* are so sad and personal, they still cannot be told.

The Eisodus

(As Opposed to Exodus—
Back to Egypt!)

ANWAR Sadat had been in Jerusalem. Both he and Begin said, "No more war!" Sadat affectionately kissed Golda Meir on the cheek. A tough peace had been negotiated.

We arrived on another temple tour to Israel. We visited Yamit in the Northern Sinai, the beautiful, architecturally innovative city Israel had built for settlers in the hot dune sands on the shore of the Mediterranean. Now Israel had to return the entire Sinai desert: the airbases, the newly discovered and immensely lucrative oil fields, the romantic tip of the great Sinai peninsula called Sharm El Sheikh, the settlements, the small towns, the villas, the monasteries of Santa Katerina, the wonderful archaeological discoveries. All of it.

Our bus was sharply inspected by Israeli Defense Force soldiers. There had been trouble with Israelis, not with Arabs. Many Israelis had to be forcibly evicted from their homes in the Sinai by the army, for the sake of peace on the southern border with Egypt. Only the military and government officials were permitted in and only tourists were allowed to get through to see what had been the fruits of the mighty Six-Day Conquest of 1967. Enormous restitution payments were given by the Israeli government to resettle and repatriate the Israeli Sinai dwellers to homes within the "Green Line."

By the time we had driven through the Negev to Eilat, Israel's bustling Red Sea resort, all the Sinai was in Egypt's hands.

Our bus driver on that trip was a quiet, rather sleepy-eyed, tired-looking veteran of the Egged bus service named Shmuel. He must have known his usual routes in the North very well. But here in the South, he often drove our excellent Israeli guide to near madness with his wrong turns, his inattentiveness, and the impression that he was asleep at the wheel. We had traversed in safety some highly dangerous, curvy, narrow mountain roads in the North and in the crags of the Aravah in the South so we knew he wasn't asleep. He just looked like he was.

One evening we had finished a grand local Red Sea fish dinner at a floating restaurant and were on our way back to the hotel, a gorgeous structure in Taba. Just beyond Taba was the renewed Sinai border with Egypt. We had eaten and had drunk of wine "that maketh glad the heart of humankind." We were joking and laughing and not paying attention to the roads. Apparently, neither was Shmuel. He drove right through the boundary line with Egypt. Suddenly sirens blew, searchlights went on, soldiers with rifles and machine guns appeared as armored jeeps bristling with weaponry surrounded us. Soldiers came forth armed and ready. They were in uniform: two different kinds of uniform: IDF and Egyptian.

We were halted. We were searched. We had to produce official papers, passenger lists, itineraries and passports. Shmuel's face bore a sickening smile. It was not a smile of joy or triumph but one of embarrassment, defeat. An "I wish I were not here" smile.

Contrary to the instruction of the Torah, Shmuel had taken us back to Egypt. It was hours, after a thorough inspection of our papers and a search of every cranny of the bus, afore, behind, inside, underneath, and our bags as well, before we could turn around and proceed the 50 or so yards back to our luxurious Israeli hotel.

Visiting Israel and being responsible for 40 or so New Yorkers is always a tenuous proceeding.

Visiting Egypt was an exciting adventure we didn't need.

Needless to say, there were always a few whiners on our tours whom I would have loved to leave behind in the Egyptian desert.

"Softhearted and Softheaded"

A WELL-KNOWN reporter from The New York Times called me. When first contacted, I had no notion of his professional journalistic celebrity. A noted war correspondent and a literary prize-winning author of books on the psychological impact of war on the human community and collective psyche, he was also the son of a minister.

An advance press release of my pending retirement had passed his desk. His editors were excited about a proposal he had put together: a ten-part series of articles that dealt with each of the Ten Commandments in a contemporary setting illustrating modern belief. The series would run for the ten days before Christmas.

He came to my apartment to interview me. I tried to be explicit concerning my non-anthropomorphic approach to Jewish theology. He asked me to suggest a family in the congregation whose struggle with tragedy had made them open to maverick religious thought, but who also had not rejected their involvement in religious institutional life. Our task was to open up candidly to him in an interview and present our heartfelt rejection of the anthropomorphic implications of the First of the Ten Commandments: "I, the Eternal, am your God who brought you out of the Land of Egypt, the house of bondage." (Exodus 20:2)

The connection between the bereaved couple and the First Commandment was the philosophical rejection of the idea that God intervenes in human history, that God did not will the death of their 9-year-old daughter, nor physically or mystically bring Hebrew slaves out of the bondage of Egypt. This was the concept of God that I taught and still hold. If one does believe in the notion of "divine intervention," then it must be conceded that the deity is at fault for some strange, destructive, inexplicable things.

That first interview took place in June 2001. We set up another appointment for September 13, 2001. As the world knows, the events of 9/11/01 changed the world. He cancelled the appointment. I saw his byline on articles dispatched from some of the brutal "hot spots" of the world. He was a busy man who experienced and wrote of some of the great struggles on our planet. I assumed that our mutual project was an item of the past.

Over a year went by. In late November of 2002, an urgent phone call: "Let's get together," he said, "my editors are excited about the project."

We convened a meeting in my apartment. He led the session with a gentleness and kindliness that made it easy for us to speak. The bereaved couple that had lost their nine-year-old daughter years ago spoke as their tears flowed. The rain outside added to the memory and melancholy inside. It was like a group psychotherapy session. I had never seen the loving father cry as easily as he did that night.

Then we discussed our assigned Commandment, that we agreed was not a command per se, but a theological statement that God acts in history and the Exodus from the slavery of Egypt was the will, the intervention, the "doing" of God.

I asserted bluntly that I rejected that theology. So did the couple, but none of us wanted, in any way, to be separated from the communal experience of the Jewish people, from the sense of history of the "House of Israel" or from our synagogue experiences.

I went on to say that one may do this within the framework of Jewish life and thought. It is only a logical response for many of us torn apart by the Holocaust. Among the six million Jewish lives destroyed were well over a million children under the age of 14.

Elie Wiesel, the Nobel Prize winner and the supreme articulate and eloquent Holocaust survivor, has said: "In contemplation of the Holocaust one must turn either to suicide, madness, or God." The thrust of his poetic eloquence is clear, but any Jew can go on, as did Job and pick up the scattered and broken pieces of existence.

Many friends and family across the continent and beyond read the article. Most agreed with us. Some didn't.

I was accused of being both softhearted and softheaded by a Roman Catholic priest. That priest, a man of letters and righteous theology, read my religious philosophy, appreciated my compassion but not my theology and in his letter to the editor, clearly didn't like it.

I felt complimented by his comment on my "soft heart." I could not help but laugh about my "soft head."

A Hindu, A Mitnaged, and Three Chasidim

THEY never shoplifted; they never crossed against the traffic light; they did not "do drugs." They were well educated, diligent in their studies and professions, but needed religious structure in their lives.

The patriarch Abraham was an exemplary prototype. He heard the call, the unembellished, simple directive: "Get out of your land, your birthplace, your father's house to a land which I will show you..." Abraham was the first Hebrew, "ivri", a term implying that like some of my students, Abraham had "passed over the line" in another direction.

The Hindu

THE ONE who became a Hindu had not grown up in our congregation but studied under the tutelage of a colleague and friend of another Reform temple in the suburbs. His parents moved into Manhattan and brought their heartache with them. No amount of talking, counseling, coaxing or pleading, even with experts on cult behavior could keep this young man from renouncing his Judaism and officially adopting the Hindu faith.

With as much gentleness as I could express, I asked him if I could bless him before he "left the fold."

I could see the fear descend upon his face. He knew that my offer was sincere, but he was just not sure, so he said he would return in a few days with an answer for me, as well as for himself. I suspect that he wanted to consult with his "guru." Whatever consultation he received had strengthened his resolve. He would not be blessed by a Rabbi, even if the blessing were simply an innocent wish for well-being and a farewell.

Years later, I officiated at the wedding of his sister. Our eyes met during the gathering a number of times. Each time I approached him, he quietly walked in the other direction.

When I think of him today I oscillate between two extreme feelings: the wish that I had grabbed him by the shoulders and said the Talmudic dictum, "Yisrael, Af Al Pi She-chata, Yisrael." "Even though one had gone astray, one born a Jew will always be a Jew!" or that I'd had the instinct to look into his eyes and cry for him and the deep pain of his parents.

The Mitnaged

STEWART HAD been born into our temple, a faithful child of our synagogue even before I became its Senior Rabbi. He was a wonderful human being: loving, gentle, sweet, intelligent, loyal. He truly loved the synagogue, his family, and his religious background.

Shortly after he had enrolled at a top Midwestern university, his parents were divorced. It was not a "nice" divorce. There was surprise, pain, and bitterness.

I believe that Stewart could not reconcile his own pain for an abandoned mother, a father who remarried a very young non-Jewish woman very quickly, and a secure and stable home life that seemed to have been shattered. He found his own new, stable restructuring.

He had already joined the Campus Hillel but now became totally a part of its scope of activities.

In years gone by, Hillel had been the "territory" for "progressive" (Reform or liberal-Conservative) rabbis. But it became far more lucrative for such rabbis to serve the swelling congregations all over the country. In a sense, many Hillels were then "taken over" by Orthodox Rabbis. This was so at Stewart's college. The rabbi there was part of the vestige of an orthodox Jewish movement that had arisen in the 18th Century to stand as a bulwark against the rapid proliferation of the Chasidic movement. The Rabbinic leaders called themselves "Mitnagdim", which means "the opposers." While Chasidism was filled with emotion and song and dance, a Judaism that was easily reached by both the elite learned and the unlearned masses, the "Mitnagdim" adhered to a stiff, very rigid, pious, restrained orthodoxy that did not lose its composure, steadfastness or dignity. Extreme learning was its highest value. Stewart matriculated from the university, and immediately proceeded to spend eight years of meticulous Talmudic study at the Mitnaged seminary in Skokie, Illinois. He would not be ordained till he was deemed ready and it took eight post-college years for that to happen.

He had grown tall and physically imposing, but that stature belied the continuing gentleness and loving-kindness of his being. The beautiful aspect of Stewart's existence, no matter how indoctrinated he was in this extreme form of Jewish life, is that he never lost his love for his own temple or his Reform Jewish background.

He took a similarly oriented wife, and became rabbi at a "centrist-Orthodox" congregation in Eastern Canada. He always re-visited New York, his family, and his rabbi. He was beloved, in a way that totally deserved love. Our temple security guard was often a little puzzled by the tall, shaggily bearded man with the wide-brimmed black hat who visited me from time to time.

I recall vividly the last time we talked. Before he left, we embraced warmly and said goodbye. I wish that I could use my tears to write for posterity the next few lines.

It was a stormy, dreadful night in northeastern Canada. Stewart began his vacation by packing his car with his belongings to join his wife who was serving as the nutritionist at a summer camp in the beautiful Canadian wilderness.

The road was covered with slippery wet leaves. The car lurched off the road, the gasoline tank exploded. Little was left of his body.

Quite simply, everyone who knew him, as well as myself, could not bear the news. The grief was public and palpable. The ceremony could not take place in our temple, because Stewart's rabbinic mentors would never enter a Reform Synagogue. We compromised on a large commercial Manhattan chapel.

I think it may have been the first time in Jewish history that a "Brisker" (a Mitnaged Rabbi from a family that originated in the Village of Brisk in Eastern Europe) co-officiated with a Reform Rabbi.

All was solemn, sad and peaceful. His "Brisker" colleagues did not call him Stewart. To them he was "Reb Shloimey."

The weather at the cemetery approached nearly 100 degrees

Fahrenheit. We shoveled the grave till a small mound appeared above the surface of the surrounding earth.

I have never really emotionally said "goodbye" to Stewart because I never really wanted to.

His mother endowed a bookshelf in my study that holds her gift of the entire Babylonian Talmud. A small bronze plaque beneath it bears his name.

We say Kaddish in front of it in remembrance of Stewart from year-to-year. Though the memory of the righteous is a blessing, I would prefer to feel the living embrace.

Three Chasidim

OY THE Chasidim! They so often give me tsuris (woes). I can't count the times I've been gently and politely accosted to say the prayers, put on tallit and tefillin, invited to study, and ended up engaged in long tumultuous dialogue, particularly on El-Al flights to and from Israel. But it also happens on the streets of midtown, downtown, uptown Manhattan and even near my country place off the famous Route #7 in the Litchfield Hills.

I could live with all their "accosting" and charmingly intrusive stubbornness, but it has been hard to make peace with their luring to their midst three of "my kids" who had been students in our temple school of Judaism.

One became a lawyer, bright, alert, and brilliant in her work. When she came to talk to me about Judaism and religion in general, I was simply not aware of the extent to which she had already been indoctrinated into the life of the Lubavitcher Chasidim. Her pattern of life had led to a lifestyle extremely different from her family and home. I know that I poured my heart out to her about my love of Judaism. I loved what could be the passion and freedom of Liberal Judaism and I wanted her to understand and share my enthusiasm. As I look back, perhaps I talked too much. But she seemed to be attentive to what I had to say, almost trying to be lured back to the intellectual ambience into which she had been born.

Although she listened, her decision had already been made. Eventually she became betrothed and married in a "pre-arranged" match, a procedure that was the norm for her adopted religious community.

It was my bittersweet honor to advise and direct her parents in the ways that they should deal with her, both emotionally and on the level of mundane matters that included visitation at her home or return visits to theirs. Kashrut (dietary laws) and modesty were the entryways to her life.

It's amazing to note the things supremely astonished parents can adapt to if they love their child.

Another Lubavitcher who graduated from my classrooms was a young man whose brilliance bordered on the level of genius. Apparently no one could have scored higher than the perfect grades on his SATs. But there was a price that was paid for this brilliance, among other things the price of parental pain. He chastised. He ran away. He disappeared for days on end. He would harangue his fellow students at secular school and Temple school. He would "entrap" his teachers at both with dialogue, conversation, and confrontation, a mode he even applied to his Rabbi. But to his disappointment, I believe, he never got me angry. I listened. I was sympathetic. I asked of him only that he stay calm and kind. Whether it was through medication, counseling, or psychotherapy, he settled down but he settled down with beard, payas, tsitsis and "Rebbes."

Lubavitcher Chasidism gave him the structure his soul sought. Though this resolution was not the one that I desired, I hope it lasts throughout a peaceful life.

The third Manhattan Chasid was a truly sweet, calm, almost transcendentally spiritual teenager who had been extremely loyal to his Jewish studies. His father was an ordinary "marginal" Jew who had married a non-Jewish woman. I instructed her long after their children were born and officiated at her conversion to Judaism.

It seemed to me the young man's "conversion" to a more extreme form of Judaism was far more visceral than intellectual. Reform Jewish observance, though a stimulating entryway for him, a source of intellectual inspiration and warm camaraderie (he had even served as president of our high school Temple Youth Group) was not enough for him. He needed more in the way of ritual identity and orthodox "grounding."

He too was married in a pre-arranged match, but at an extraordinarily young age.

I met his parents recently by chance. There was warm affection all round. They informed me that their son, the Lubavitcher Chasid, was soon to be a father. The baby would be their first grandchild.

Some day when I am ready to write the sequel to my "Tales," I will have met and interviewed the surviving "strayers." Till then: *haltzich oop!*

(Don't hold your breath!)

A Major Discovery
On the Major Deegan

G ERTA and Hilda were elderly sisters, utterly devoted to each
other and to their brother, Willy. All had been born long ago in
Germany and arrived in this country when very young, and all spoke
English quite well with a touch of a German accent that was charming.
Each one had been successful and in spite of deep familial attachment,
each was totally, stubbornly independent.

At an early point in my rabbinic tenure in their midst, the two sisters,
now both widowed, came with me on our first temple tour to Israel.
They were excellent travelers: neat, always punctual, never in need of
special attention, and constantly appreciative of every sight and sound
on the trip. The three siblings loved to laugh. Whether in English, or
momentarily lapsing into German, they had easily aroused smiles and
constantly teased each other, especially about their increasing old-age
infirmities. They possessed a sweet "continental" charm and it was
always a pleasure to be with them.

As the days passed, Gerta, the oldest, became very ill. Yet even when
I visited the hospital, I found them engaging and ready to smile and
laugh.

After months of decline, Gerta died. The funeral was arranged and it
was my honor to officiate at the ceremony. I was also to accompany Hilda
and Willy to the family plot at our temple cemetery in Westchester.

Only a few people were at the funeral home ceremony and only one
limousine followed the hearse.

Hilda, Willy, and I were conversing in the back seat when suddenly the driver said "Oh my!" and swerved off the Major Deegan Expressway as he followed the careening hearse off the highway onto a small side street in the Bronx.

We pulled over and stopped. The driver of the hearse stepped out of his vehicle and walked quickly to our car. His face was ashen and he could hardly speak.

"I just turned around a moment ago," he said breathlessly, "and there is no coffin in my hearse."

We agreed that he would drive the hearse back to the funeral home in Manhattan, and we would continue in the limo at a slow, leisurely pace to the cemetery in Westchester and await his arrival there.

Inwardly, I was very disturbed but I felt that I had to make the best of a terrible, unforgivable situation. When we were all seated and our car was back on the Major Deegan, I said, "You know, Gerta had such a good sense of humor-she would have loved this!"

To my relief, both Hilda and Willy agreed. They offered their repeated Germanic "Yah Yahs" and laughed with me, in spite of the hurtful carelessness of the funeral home.

We "Yah-Yahed" and laughed and talked with animation all the way to the gates of the cemetery. Moments after we entered, a black station wagon swerved in behind us carrying the missing coffin.

Ah, what timing! What excellent recovery and good fortune!

I entered the cemetery office with the driver. The cemetery manager quite calmly and efficiently asked for the necessary papers for burial. The driver of the station wagon with the coffin said, "Oh my God, the papers are in the hearse and the hearse is in Manhattan."

The cemetery manager stated quite coldly, "Then there will be no burial without the proper papers!"

It was at that moment that my inward emotional churning boiled over. I said, "There will be a burial and there will be a burial *now*! You can't do this to these people. They have reacted sweetly and kindly long enough! You will eventually get your papers but the ceremony and burial will take place *now*!"

"Oh, no it won't!" said the manager.

"Oh, yes it will!" said the Rabbi, "Even if I have to roll the coffin to the grave and fill it in myself—NOW!"

I gestured to the two drivers to follow me. The manager was furious.

We exited his office, went to the cars, and quickly drove up the hill and around the curve to the waiting, open grave.

I did not let on to Hilda and Willy what was taking place. I led them to the open grave. One of the drivers and I were moving to try to lift the coffin. It was heavy. There was no gurney. Perhaps righteous, intemperate indignation had led me to error. We began to tug. Nothing moved.

At that moment, the hearse appeared, almost as if in a cloud of dust, containing the hearse driver, the manager, the papers, and a rolling gurney. We proceeded as properly planned. The coffin found its resting place. I found the correct page in my manual. Hilda and Willy found "closure."

On the return trip, we couldn't help laughing and "Yah-Yahing" over the morning's events.

A House of Prayer for All People

THE main entrance to the Synagogue is right on street level. Even with newly devised security procedures, anyone can enter. Just about all have a right to come in and need no search or surveillance but the practically open access has often kept matters very lively.

I recall the unexpected and unnerving behavior of a single, middle-aged gentleman who suffered from Tourette's Syndrome. He came two weeks in a row, the first visit a Friday night service when he started to passionately shriek "Adonai! Adonai!", one of the Hebrew words for God, and a week later when he began to shout words from the prayer book in the midst of a huge Bar Mitzvah ceremony on Shabbat morning. Fortunately, the ushers were effective and kind.

The same kind of malady afflicted another young man who was a medical school student and attended services often in order to encourage his fiancée's course of conversion to Judaism. He was studying medicine in order to become an expert in precisely the illness that beset his life. He urged me to explain his outbursts and symptoms during the service to the congregants so people would understand and forgive. He and his fiancée were always sweetly grateful when I did so and the congregants understood.

We have been "dropped-in-on" by Princes of the Catholic Church, great and internationally known performers of the stage, television, and motion pictures, the mayor of the city, athletes of great accomplishment and renown, professors and presidents of the nation's universities, builders of the city, titans of industry, ambassadors and judges from

City-Civil to State Appeals to State and U.S. Supreme Courts, Senators, Governors, writers, dancers, choreographers, and perhaps most easily remembered of all, people who were "mentally challenged."

I mean no disrespect or cynicism. A basic feeling of compassion underlies my approach to human beings. But sometimes the antics of "challenged" persons simply do not leave the memory.

One young man came to services for years. He sat silently and attentively and never spoke with anyone. He lived in the outpatient section of a hospital for the "mentally challenged" on the other side of the East River. It was a long, complicated trip for him to come to services. He loved to come and rarely missed a week. He always joined the collation after Friday night services and came through the receiving line to shake hands with us, but always in silence.

Until one day those who attended to him must have changed his medication and the "silent one" became extremely verbose.

He began to tell us extensively about his background. We listened with care. The narratives increased. He crossed the line. In the midst of the hectic setting after Friday night services, he began to tell us far more than we wanted to know.

When we encouraged him to make a private appointment, he always turned us down. He then began to contact us by telephone, always asking about the Friday night service. Who would preach? What time did the service begin? Would there be a collation? Did the Rabbi have a sermon title for him? All this was tolerable but when he began to call me at home and directed these questions to my wife and children, a sense of "compassion surfeit" was reached.

Just as we were about to enact a mild sort of discipline, the effort became unnecessary. Those who attended him, probably suffering from his extreme verbosity far more than we at the Temple, must have administered a different or former medication and suddenly, again, he no longer talked. At least now, he smiled, often and easily. After about a year of silence and smiling, he disappeared.

Another pathetic soul brought his tuxedo, on a hanger, with him to services. He insisted that I officiate at his wedding immediately. I did not respond positively or enthusiastically. "Where is your wife-to-be?" I asked him. His response was that she had disappeared and it was my duty to find her and to join them in marriage. When turned away, gently, he never returned.

Prominent in my memory was the gray-haired lady who came to services on Friday nights for years. She was dressed conventionally, a bit threadbare and worn but acceptable, except for the enormous bunny slippers on her feet.

She too was silent for years. She pursued her special Temple project and bothered no one; she always brought with her a polishing cloth for brass and would shine up all the brass door handles she could find in the lobby and on the doors of the sanctuary. She worked steadily until each service began and then sat attentively. She was silent. She always looked as though she was going to say something but never did, until one Friday night.

I had received a call from the Executive Vice President of the Central Conference of American Rabbis. Cesar Chavez, the noted founder and leader of the United Farm Workers of America, was in town and wanted to address the New York City religious community. His organization was urging a boycott against a certain brand of broccoli. The owners of those farms were not paying the migrant pickers adequately and were forcing them to live in conditions of squalid poverty. It sounded like "The Grapes of Wrath" all over again. I agreed to have him come, much to the consternation of some of my fiercely right-wing board members.

Chavez spoke. One could feel the man's sincerity and could feel, in response, the empathy of the members of the Temple. Sympathy came from every direction but one.

At the social hour afterwards, the silent lady in the huge bunny slippers approached me. She came up very close to me, truly in my face. She was very disturbed about the evening and now she was ready to speak.

Her words to me, in a harsh German accent, were: "Iss behoccoli gut for ze pipple?"

I was nonplussed. I knew of broccoli's healthful vitamins and anti-oxidants. Its benefits were not really the point of the evening. She repeated her question, the exact words again and again, getting stronger, louder:

"Iss behoccoli gut for ze pipple?"

I finally said, "No!"

I never saw her again.

Mistaken Identity

SOMETIMES, in a clergy household, there is an urgent need for "comfort food."

Such was the situation shortly before Rosh Hashanah one year. A terrible, unspeakable tragedy had taken place in the life of a family in the Temple membership. It involved three deaths and the media had given the occurrence great unwanted attention. I will refrain from the details of the story because I will no way bring added hurt to the pain of the survivors. Their suffering and grief has been unimaginable.

I became deeply involved with the family and was scheduled to conduct the service and eulogy. The composition of a eulogy and the selection of appropriate passages for the service were a challange unlike any I had before or since.

The night before the funeral, I chose readings only from the Book of Job. Of all 36 books of "Tanach," "The Hebrew Bible," Job and Ecclesiastes are, for me, the most directly oriented to the reality and pain of the human condition.

I made my selections and wrote the eulogy words that I would say, and I felt depleted, as did Meryl, my wife, who had listened to me speak them.

We agreed that we needed some sustenance.

I left our apartment building and crossed the street to a small, independent grocery which was still open. My purchase of ice cream and cake were in a grocery bag in my arms and, still thinking of the daunting task ahead of me in the morning, I walked along one of those sidewalk patches filled with Belgian granite blocks which would ordinarily be flat and surround a tree. The blocks were not flat. I was not paying attention to footing. I fell—the bag flew ahead of me to the road and I tried to cushion the headlong fall with my left hand. I did,, but I sustained a severe cut in the fleshy area between my thumb and forefinger.

I gathered up the comfort food and crossed safely to our building and home. One good look at the wound convinced us that stitches were needed. We called the emergency room at the hospital and reported there immediately. Stitches were inserted and we paid the bill for forty-five dollars.

Fortunately, all the bleeding soon ceased and I was able to carry out the heartbreaking task of leading the service, giving the eulogy, and officiating at the burials.

Rosh Hashanah, with all its excitement, pageantry, shofar-blowing, and sermons of inspiration, followed the day after.

A day or two had passed when Meryl informed me that she had called upon the superintendent of the building that fronted the sidewalk with the disarranged granite blocks. When she explained that her husband had fallen and sustained injury that required emergency room attention—stitches for the open wound—she had shown him the paid hospital bill. It seemed to her that he could not write a check for forty-five dollars fast enough to reimburse us.

The following evening the weather was balmy and pleasant. We took a late evening walk and crossed the street. Meryl pointed out to me the building in which the "super" had quickly written out the check.

I stopped suddenly. For a tense moment, I couldn't say a word. Then it poured out. I said, "Sweetheart, that's not the building where I fell! It's the one next to it!" Both buildings had tree squares with granite blocks in disarray!

What to do?

We found the super and, to his great surprise, gave the money back.

For years the incident got more and more hilarious as we told it to others!

Who Are You?

WHEN I announced my plan to depart from the Village Temple to the Temple uptown, there was both anger and sadness.

I thought it would be appropriate to tell the children at Sunday School about it. I had led the Sunday School assembly for the entire six years that I had been both Rabbi and school principal.

I tried to make the announcement as gentle as I could. There were some faces with tears, and some without expression.

One little girl, whose family had recently joined, listened intently. She leaned forward. She raised her hand. I called on her and she said, "I don't think I know who you are!"

That statement was medicinal, therapeutic. It put a great deal of emotion into proper prospective. It had the power to obliterate whatever solipsism to which one may have been prone in a changing professional situation in which most of the emotions are within the breast of one person: oneself.

Bravo, new little girl! I have quoted you often through many years of rabbinic leadership.

A Tale to End the "Tales"

THE congregation's battle was picked up by every newspaper and television news network. The New York Times, that declares it publishes "All the News That's Fit to Print", put the internal congregational struggle on the front page. It may well be in that particular time period in late 1970 to early 1971 that very little was happening in the world, but the "rabbi fight" seemed to capture worldwide attention. It was not the struggle of the Village Temple, but of the temple on the Upper East Side where I had previously served as Assistant Rabbi for three years.

My predecessor there had retired. The pulpit committee scoured the country to fill the vacancy with a suitable successor. They had eliminated all previous assistants from eligibility even though we had been called in for multiple interviews. That was their first mistake.

[During the search period, at an annual convention of the CCAR, the Central Conference of Reform Rabbis, a large group of colleagues and I were seated at a big table having lunch. The roar of laughter that filled the dining room was occasioned by the revelation that the Temple had interviewed every one of us.]

The pulpit committee was far too large and unwieldy and the whole process of the search had gone on for far too long a time. The "searchers" had grown stale.

At last, a rabbinic candidate was offered the position. He seemed to fit the needs of the search committee and the congregation. I knew him as a politically conservative colleague who had published a sermon about the correctness of U.S. involvement in Vietnam.

But when he began his tenure that summer at the Upper East Side temple, his physical appearance had changed; his hair, both front and back, seemed to reach down to his belt. The New York Times later described him as "the hippie Rabbi". This change had a decidedly mixed impact on the membership of the Temple.

Everything came to a climax at a congregational meeting whose only subject was whether or not to keep this rabbi in his position. Because of the large turnout, the meeting was held in the main sanctuary.

The reports filtered downtown to me. The meeting was terrible and, for some, terrifying. Limousines had been sent to gather elderly voters. An archaic line in the Temple constitution and by-laws no one had heard of until that meeting barred anyone younger than thirty from casting a valid vote! The restriction was enforced. Scores of people swore they would never again enter the Sanctuary. The Rabbi's side lost by six votes.

"Rabbi fights" have taken place in the Reform, Conservative and Orthodox movements for decades. They are not new or rare. There is something emotionally charged in Temple politics; one can feel it even at the most ordinary board meetings. Internal struggles are not unusual. There is no hierarchy in Reform Judaism. Each congregation is totally independent, whether true "internal democracy" is achieved or not.

The great difference in this unfortunate struggle was that a certain faction released information to the media, and the media indulged in a crazed, albeit temporary, "feeding frenzy". All the TV news stations and even the stately New York Times participated.

After the ouster, the retired Senior Rabbi came back to the pulpit to serve temporarily.

I had been happy downtown. The Village was my territory. We had shared some meaningful success and some very happy times, but now I felt my "destiny" was calling.

Still, it was a scary time for me and for my family. The success of the Village Temple felt very good, but a true challenge was beckoning.

When I made my decision to answer the challenge, I spent the longest day of my life informing at least a dozen members of the Board and officers of my decision to leave and to present my request to do so face-to-face at their offices all over town.

There was no question in my mind that after the very first visit, the word was passed before I could make subsequent visits, but I was determined to do this on as personal a level as possible. I got home very late that night.

On Friday night, April 30th, I gave my "goodbye sermon" downtown. And on Saturday morning, May 1st, I gave my "hello sermon" uptown. For me, it was the most emotionally, professionally spirit-wrenching Shabbat I have ever known.

For the next thirty years I was the Rabbi uptown and not once, ever, did I return to be on the pulpit downtown. Certain personal relationships did continue.

Perhaps the whole transformation could be summed up in the ambivalent feelings of my seven-year-old son: "O Dad," said he, with the tears flowing, "You're not quitting that little temple, are you?"

But the following morning he bounced back with a sheaf of papers with his own hand-drawings: "Dad, I made this game for you. It's called 'The Road to the New Temple.' I know everything will be okay." He was right.

It was more than okay, after years of putting the pieces back together.

The photograph and article on the front page of the New York Times read: "Uptown Synagogue Engages New Rabbi." The article emphasized (as if it mattered) that I was a former U.S. Marine Corps Chaplain and that I was tall, husky, and clean-shaven.

A new era of "tales" had begun.

Epilogue

I HAVE recalled and transcribed many of these incidents because I wanted to share them. I felt they might offer engaging reading.

There is also another purpose. I want people to know how I feel about certain things, about human beings, about religious institutions, about rabbinic work, and about the openness of Jewish theological pathways.

I have felt for decades that the modern and postmodern movements in Jewish life need an increasing sense of traditionalist ritual expression, but one that made sense and was not exclusivist or overbearing and at the same time, had a deep sense of theological flexibility.

Theological exploration is not new to Judaism. For me, Judaism opened a way of thinking that negated the concept of an anthropomorphic divine being (i.e., "a personal God") millennia ago. For me, and for many, many Jews, God remains a question mark. The idea of an omnipotent being, a personal God, who made demands and sought righteousness faded away thousands of years ago and was ultimately mangled by the evil of the Holocaust. Far too many phrases of the old and new prayer books speak in anthropomorphic and anthropopathic terms. For me, the books are in need of constant editing and updating.

A non-anthropomorphic understanding of God can be found in streams of Jewish thought from the book of Exodus, the writings of Job and Ecclesiastes, the Aramaic translations of Onkelos (which struggle to avoid anthropomorphic limitations about God), the allegories of Philo, the philosophic treatises of Maimonides, the pantheistic approach of Spinoza, and the pre—and post-Holocaust thinking of Kaplan, Fackenheim, Rubenstein, and others.

I have felt deeply that while some people have been upset by my "non-

traditionalist" theological approach, far, far more have been comforted
and gratified by it.

Tragedy has been everywhere and connection to the Jewish
community should not be obstructed by a notion of God that is
irrelevant, rigid, and puerile in regard to "the human condition" and
especially in regard to the horrible happenings to Jews in the course of
history. I don't need a concept of God to ratify the meaning of the social
contract for an orderly or even democratic society, nor do I need God in
order to hope and work for a better world. The idea of a personal God,
for me, raises more questions than answers.

For me, the world is God. The universe is God. Life is God. And
beyond all that we can possibly know there is the unknown and the
unknowable, the mystery of existence, the profound, unknowable
infinity of the universe, and the universe of universes.

I can call out my prayer, hope, poetry and song to that mystery, to
the mystic connection, to philosophical seeking and understanding,
and to the community of my Jewish people. Our thoughts can go in
dozens of different directions; we can be coming from a multitude
of places and the synagogue can be wide, big, strong, and embracing
enough to include us all.

In a philosophical approach like this, a specific term must be
addressed: "covenant." On numerous occasions and in theological
discussions I have witnessed how important this term is to many of
my colleagues and fellow Jews. "Covenant", broadly and simply, refers
to the contract between the Children of Israel and God: "You will
be our God; we will be your people", the two-sided expression of the
commitment, simply put, the contract.

In addition to an acknowledgment of the historical fact that the
Jewish people have been more faithful to the covenant than has God,
there is, for me and others, the disturbing comprehension that the entire
concept of "covenant/contract" (a binding of two parties) is mundanely
anthropomorphic. A non-personal God, a "pantheistic" notion of God,
cannot be molded into a two-way pact in which one partner is totally
absent or abstract.

I can redeem some of this terminology by speaking not of "covenant"
but of a sense of "covenantedness", a commitment that many Jews feel
spiritually, philosophically, and communally binds them to the history
and destiny of the House of Israel. That sense of faithful belonging,

of mystical, benevolent peoplehood, is both physical and metaphysical, both natural and supernatural, both factual and rhapsodic. Though I cannot accept the notion of covenant on philosophical grounds, my heart and mind are deeply attuned to the idea of covenantedness that is rooted in history, fact, and emotion.

Having served as a congregational rabbi for well over forty years, I feel within the deepest part of my being that this sense of covenantedness to which I gave most of my life was fulfilling, meaningful, and holy.

About the Author

Rabbi Harvey Tattelbaum was born in Boston, Massachusetts, and was educated at Harvard University and the Hebrew College, which he attended simultaneously, and he graduated with honors from both in the same week of June, 1955.

He was awarded a traveling fellowship for a year's study at the Hebrew University in Jersualem. Upon return to the U.S., he enrolled in the Hebrew College Union College (Jewish Institute of Religion of N.Y.) where he was ordained a Rabbi in 1960.

Drafted into the military by his own Rabbinic organization (CCAR), he served as a Navy Chaplain assigned to the U.S. Marines at Parris Island Marine Corps Recruit Depot, SC, for two years.

Upon leaving active duty, he was appointed assistant Rabbi at Temple Shaaray Tefila in Manhattan for three years and then served as Rabbi of "The Village Temple" (Congregation B'nai Israel of Greenwich Village) for six years and then returned to Shaaray Tefila as Senior Rabbi for the remaining thirty years of his career.

He is married to the former Meryl Herrmann of N.Y.C. and they have three married children and seven grandchildren.

They both adore the excitement and vitality of Manhattan as well as their lakeside Connecticut country home where most of the "village tales" were actually written.

CPSIA information can be obtained at www.ICGtesting.com
Printed in the USA
BVOW071714091111

275680BV00001B/347/P

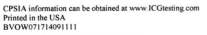